Shakespeare
THE ANIMATED TALES

ROMEO AND JULIET

HAMLET

TWELFTH NIGHT

A MIDSUMMER NIGHT'S DREAM

MACBETH

THE TEMPEST

ABRIDGED BY
LEON GARFIELD

HEINEMANN · LONDON

Shakespeare The Animated Tales is a multinational venture conceived by S4C, Channel 4 Wales. Produced in Russia, Wales and England, the series has been financed by S4C, the BBC and HIT Communications (UK), Christmas Films and Soyuzmultfilm (Russia), Home Box Office (USA) and Fujisankei (Japan).

Academic Panel
Professor Stanley Wells
Dr Rex Gibson

Academic Co-ordinator
Roy Kendall

Educational Adviser
Michael Marland

Publishing Editor and Co-ordinator
Jane Fior

Book Design
Fiona Macmillan

Animation Director for *The Tempest*
Stanislav Sokolov of Soyuzmultfilm Studios, Moscow

Animation Director for *Twelfth Night*
Maria Muat of Soyuzmultfilm Studios, Moscow

Animation Director for *Macbeth*
Nikolai Serebriakov of Soyuzmultfilm Studios, Moscow

Animation Director for *A Midsummer Night's Dream*
Robert Saakianz of Christmas Joint Venture, Moscow

Animation Director for *Romeo and Juliet*
Efim Gambourg of Soyuzmultfilm Studios, Moscow

Animation Director for *Hamlet*
Natalia Orlova of Soyuzmultfilm Studios, Moscow

Series Producer and Director
Dave Edwards of The Dave Edwards Studio Ltd, Cardiff

Executive Producers
Christopher Grace
Elizabeth Babakhina
Igor Markozyan

William Heinemann Ltd
Michelin House, 81 Fulham Road
London SW3 6RB
LONDON · MELBOURNE · AUCKLAND
First published 1992
Text and illustrations © Shakespeare Animated Films Limited
Christmas Joint Venture and Soyuzmultfilm 1992
ISBN 0 434 96228 7
Printed and bound in the UK by BPCC Hazell Books Limited

The publishers would like to thank Paul Cox for
the use of his illustration of The Globe and
the series logo illustration, Carole Kempe for
her calligraphy, Patrick Spottiswoode for his
introduction and Elizabeth Laird, Ness Wood,
Rosa Fior and Jillian Boothroyd for their help
in the production of the books.

Contents

WILLIAM SHAKESPEARE

NEXT TO GOD, A wise man once said, Shakespeare created most. In the thirty-seven plays that are his chief legacy to the world — and surely no-one ever left a richer! — human nature is displayed in all its astonishing variety.

He has enriched the stage with matchless comedies, tragedies, histories, and, towards the end of his life, with plays that defy all description, strange plays that haunt the imagination like visions.

His range is enormous: kings and queens, priests, princes and merchants, soldiers, clowns and drunkards, murderers, pimps, whores, fairies, monsters and pale, avenging ghosts 'strut and fret their hour upon the stage'. Murders and suicides abound; swords flash, blood flows, poison drips, and lovers sigh; yet there is always time for old men to talk of growing apples and for gardeners to discuss the weather.

In the four hundred years since they were written, they have become known and loved in every land; they are no longer the property of one country and one people, they are the priceless possession of the world.

His life, from what we know of it, was not astonishing. The stories that have attached themselves to him are remarkable only for their ordinariness: poaching deer, sleeping off a drinking bout under a wayside tree. There are no duels, no loud, passionate loves, no excesses of any kind. He was not one of your unruly geniuses whose habits are more interesting than their works. From all accounts, he was of a gentle, honourable disposition, a good businessman, and a careful father.

He was born on April 23rd 1564, to John and Mary Shakespeare of Henley Street, Stratford-upon-Avon. He was their third child and first son. When he was four or five he began his education at the local petty school. He left the local grammar school when he was about fourteen, in all probability to help in his father's glove-making shop. When he was eighteen, he married Anne Hathaway, who lived in a nearby village. By the time he was twenty-one, he was the father of three children, two daughters and a son.

Then, it seems, a restless mood came upon him. Maybe he travelled, maybe he was, as some say, a schoolmaster in the country; but at some time during the next seven years, he went to London and found employment in the theatre. When he was twenty-eight, he was already well enough known as an actor and playwright to excite the spiteful envy of a rival, who referred to him as 'an upstart crow'.

He mostly lived and worked in London until his mid-forties, when he returned to his family and home in Stratford, where he remained in prosperous circumstances until his death on April 23rd 1616, his fifty-second birthday.

He left behind him a widow, two daughters (his son died in childhood), and the richest imaginary world ever created by the human mind.

LEON GARFIELD

The Theatre in Shakespeare's Day

IN 1989 AN ARCHAEOLOGICAL discovery was made on the south bank of the Thames that sent shivers of delight through the theatre world. A fragment of Shakespeare's own theatre, the Globe, where many of his plays were first performed, had been found.

This discovery has fuelled further interest in how Shakespeare himself conceived and staged his plays. We know a good deal already, and archaeology as well as documentary research will no doubt reveal more, but although we can only speculate on some of the details, we have a good idea of what the Elizabethan theatre-goer saw, heard and smelt when he went to see a play by William Shakespeare at the Globe.

It was an entirely different experience from anything we know today. Modern theatres have roofs to keep out the weather. If it rained on the Globe, forty per cent of the play-goers got wet. Audiences today sit on cushioned seats, and usually (especially if the play is by Shakespeare) watch and listen in respectful silence. In the Globe, the floor of the theatre was packed with a riotous crowd of garlic-reeking apprentices, house servants and artisans, who had each paid a penny to stand for the entire duration of the play, to buy nuts and apples from the food-sellers, to refresh themselves with bottled ale, relieve themselves, perhaps, into buckets by the back wall, to talk, cheer, catcall, clap and hiss if the play did not please them.

In the galleries, that rose in curved tiers around the inside of the building, sat those who could afford to pay two pennies for a seat, and the benefits of a roof over their heads. Here, the middle ranking citizens, the merchants, the sea captains, the clerks from the Inns of Court, would sit crammed into their small eighteen inch space and look down upon the 'groundlings' below. In the 'Lords room', the rich and the great, noblemen and women, courtiers and foreign ambassadors had to pay sixpence each for the relative comfort and luxury of their exclusive position directly above the stage, where they smoked tobacco, and overlooked the rest.

We are used to a stage behind an arch, with wings on either side, from which the actors come on and into which they disappear. In the Globe, the stage was a platform thrusting out into the middle of the floor, and the audience, standing in the central yard, surrounded it on three sides. There were no wings. Three doors at the back of the stage were used for all exits and entrances. These were sometimes covered by a curtain, which could be used as a prop.

Today we sit in a darkened theatre or cinema, and look at a brilliantly lit stage or screen, or we sit at home in a small, private world of our own, watching a luminous television screen. The close-packed, rowdy crowd at the Globe, where the play started at two o'clock in the afternoon, had no artificial light to enhance their illusion. It was the words that moved them. They came to listen, rather than to see.

No dimming lights announced the start of the play. A blast from a trumpet and three sharp knocks warned the audience that the action was about to begin. In the broad daylight, the actor could see the audience as clearly as the audience could see him. He spoke directly to the crowd, and held them with his eyes, following their reactions. He could play up to the raucous laughter that greeted the comical, bawdy scenes, and gauge the emotional response to the higher flights of poetry. Sometimes he even improvised speeches of his own. He was surrounded by, enfolded by his audience.

The stage itself would seem uncompromisingly bare to our eyes. There was no scenery. No painted backdrops suggested a forest, or a castle, or the sumptuous interior of a palace. Shakespeare painted the scenery with his words, and the imagination of the audience did the rest.

Props were brought onto the stage only when they were essential for the action. A bed would be carried on when a character needed to lie on it. A throne would be let down from above when a king needed to sit on it. Torches and lanterns would suggest that it was dark, but the main burden of persuading an audience, at three o'clock in the afternoon, that it was in fact the middle of the night, fell upon the language.

Shakespeare's actors were responsible for their own costumes. They would use what was to hand in the 'tiring house' (dressing room), or supplement it out of their own pockets. Classical, medieval and Tudor clothes could easily appear side by side in the same play.

No women actors appeared on a public stage until many years after Shakespeare's death, for at that time it would have been considered shameless. The parts of young girls were played by boys. The parts of older women were played by older men.

In 1613 the Globe theatre was set on fire by a spark from a cannon during a performance of Henry VIII, and it burnt to the ground. The actors, including Shakespeare himself, dug into their own pockets and paid for it to be rebuilt. The new theatre lasted until 1642, when it closed again. Now, in the 1990s, the Globe is set to rise again as a committed band of actors, scholars and enthusiasts are raising the money to rebuild Shakespeare's theatre in its original form a few yards from its previous site.

From the time when the first Globe theatre was built until today, Shakespeare's plays have been performed in a vast variety of languages, styles, costumes and techniques, on stage, on film, on television and in animated film. Shakespeare himself, working within the round wooden walls of his theatre, would have been astonished by it all.

PATRICK SPOTTISWOODE
Director of Education,
Globe Theatre Museum

ROMEO *and* JULIET

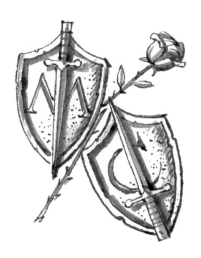

The curtain rises on old Verona, on a market-place covered over with huge umbrella-awnings that shield the busy crowded stalls from the blazing summer's sun. All of a sudden, the umbrellas quake and tumble aside to reveal, like furious insects under a stone, a frantic squabbling of mad colours. Shouts and shrieks fill the air, of fright and rage and outrage! The Montagues and the Capulets—two ancient warring families—are at each others' throats again! Stalls are wrecked, merchandise scattered and screaming children snatched out of the way by their terrified mothers.

VÒICES   Down with the Capulets! Down with the Montagues!

Benvolio, a sensible young Montague, seeks to put an end to the uproar.

BENVOLIO   Part, fools, put up your swords!

He is accosted by Tybalt, a dangerous Capulet.

TYBALT   Turn thee, Benvolio, look upon thy death!

They fight, causing more destruction to all about them.

A CITIZEN   A plague on both your houses!

Old Capulet, venerable and dignified, accompanied by his wife and a servant, appears upon the scene. At once, the old man's heart is stirred into a fury.

CAPULET   Give me my long sword, ho!

LADY CAPULET   (*restraining him*) A crutch, a crutch! Why call you for a sword?

Too late. The old man has seen his chief enemy. Old Montague and his lady approach.

CAPULET   My sword, I say! Old Montague is come!

MONTAGUE   Thou villain Capulet!

He draws his sword, but Lady Montague drags him back.

MONTAGUE   Hold me not! Let me go!

LADY MONTAGUE Thou shalt not stir one foot to seek a foe!

Trumpets sound. Soldiers and Prince Escalus enter the market-place. Enraged by the scene of civil strife that greets him, the prince shouts, at first, in vain.

PRINCE   Rebellious subjects, enemies to peace—Will they not hear?
               What ho, you men, you beasts! On pain of torture, throw your

mistempered weapons to the ground and hear the sentence of
your moved prince. (*The fighting ceases.*) Three civil brawls,
bred of an airy word, by thee, old Capulet, and Montague,
have thrice disturbed the quiet of our streets. If ever you
disturb our streets again, your lives shall pay the forfeit of the
peace. For this time all the rest depart away.

*At the Prince's words the crowd obediently disperses, leaving
ruin and the creators of it behind. Sternly, the Prince addresses
the two old men.*

PRINCE   You, Capulet, shall go along with me, and Montague, come
              you this afternoon, to know our farther pleasure in this case.

*He turns and rides away. Old Capulet and his wife follow, and
with them, the sullen Tybalt. Angrily, Lady Capulet snatches
his rapier away from him, as if depriving a naughty child of its
toy. Old Montague, his wife and Benvolio are left behind with
a stall-keeper or two, crawling about to recover scattered
possessions.*

LADY MONTAGUE   O where is Romeo, saw you him today?

BENVOLIO   Madam, underneath the grove of sycamore did I see your
                son—

MONTAGUE   —Many a morning hath he there been seen, with tears
                augmenting the fresh morning's dew, adding to clouds more
                clouds with his deep sighs . . .

BENVOLIO	My noble uncle, do you know the cause?
MONTAGUE	I neither know it, nor can learn it of him.
BENVOLIO	See where he comes!

Enter Romeo, a sad figure, moving disconsolately along a colonnade. He pauses by a column and, with his dagger, begins to incise in the stone.

BENVOLIO	*(to Montague and his wife)* So please you step aside; I'll know his grievance or be much denied.

Old Montague and his wife depart. Benvolio approaches Romeo.

BENVOLIO	Good morrow, cousin.
ROMEO	*(obscuring his knife-work)* What, is the day so young?
BENVOLIO	But new struck nine.
ROMEO	Ay me, sad hours seem long.
BENVOLIO	What sadness lengthens Romeo's hours?

For answer, Romeo reveals what he has been hiding: the name, 'Rosalyne' with an added heart. All the columns he has passed have been similarly wounded by his loving dagger.

BENVOLIO   In love?

ROMEO   Out. Out of her favour where I am in love.

Benvolio seats himself upon a step, and signs to Romeo to join him.

BENVOLIO   Be ruled by me, forget to think of her.

ROMEO   O teach me how I should forget.

BENVOLIO   By giving liberty unto thine eyes: examine other beauties.

ROMEO   (*rising*) Farewell, thou canst not teach me—

As he speaks, a puzzled figure comes into the market-place. It is a servant of the Capulets. He is studying a piece of paper. It is a list of guests invited to a feast at his master's house. Unfortunately, he cannot read. He approaches Romeo.

SERVANT   I pray sir, can you read?

ROMEO   Ay, mine own fortune in my misery.

SERVANT   Perhaps you have learned it without book.

He turns to go. Romeo detains him.

ROMEO   Stay, fellow, I can read. (*He takes the paper and begins to read.*)

ROMEO   Signor Martino and his wife and daughters; County Anselm and his beauteous sisters; the lady widow of Utruvio; Signor Placentio and his lovely nieces; Mercutio and his brother Valentine; mine uncle Capulet, his wife and daughters; my fair niece Rosalyne— (*Romeo pauses, then reads on*) —and Livia; Signor Valentio and his cousin Tybalt; Lucio and the lively Helena. (*He returns the list.*) A fair assembly. Whither should they come?

SERVANT   My master is the great rich Capulet, and if you be not of the house of Montagues, I pray come and crush a cup of wine. Rest you merry.

The servant departs with the list.

BENVOLIO   At this same ancient feast of Capulet's sups the fair Rosalyne. Go thither and with unattainted eye compare her face with some that I shall show and I will make thee think thy swan a crow.

ROMEO   One fairer than my love! The all-seeing sun ne'er saw her match!

BENVOLIO   Tut, you saw her fair, none else being by . . .

The house of the Capulets is noisy with revelry. Gorgeous guests move to and fro. Masks, masks, masks! In black and silver, scarlet and gold: snarling beast-masks, beaked bird-masks, devil-masks, and masks as pale and blank as the moon . . . all shifting, turning, nodding, while through their black slits peep eyes that burn and sparkle and shoot voluptu-ous arrows of desire . . . Old Capulet, the host, bustles about in high delight.

CAPULET   Welcome, gentlemen, ladies that have their toes unplagued with corns will walk a bout with you . . . Come, musicians, play! A hall, a hall, give room! And foot it, girls!

A stately air strikes up. Couples form, beasts and moon-faces . . . By the door stand Romeo and Benvolio. Hastily, they don their masks. Romeo's is calm and golden . . . Benvolio tries to drag Romeo into the festivities. He will not come. Mercutio, Romeo's good friend and kinsman to the prince, in a mask that reflects his lively, mocking nature, joins them. He lays an affectionate arm round Romeo's shoulder.

MERCUTIO   We must have you dance!

ROMEO   Not I, believe me. You have dancing shoes with nimble soles; I have a soul of lead.

MERCUTIO   You are a lover; borrow Cupid's wings!

ROMEO   Peace, peace, Mercutio, peace. (*Mercutio shrugs his shoulders and moves away. Romeo murmurs to himself.*) My mind misgives some consequence yet hanging in the stars shall bitterly begin his fearful date with this night's revels . . .

He gazes at the dancers: a long procession of pale moon-faces linked with lascivious beasts. Suddenly one face is seen unmasked. It is the face of a young girl and it seems to flood the world with radiance. Romeo cries out in amazement. He turns to a servant beside him.

ROMEO   What lady's that which doth enrich the hand of yonder knight?

SERVANT   I know not, sir.

ROMEO   O she doth teach the torches to burn bright. It seems she hangs upon the cheek of night as a rich jewel in an Ethiop's ear! Did my heart love till now? Forswear it, sight, for I ne'er saw true beauty till this night!

He moves towards her like one in a dream. He passes close by Tybalt . . .

TYBALT   This by his voice should be a Montague! (*He turns to a serving-boy.*) Fetch me my rapier, boy! What, dares the slave come hither—

Old Capulet, seeing that Tybalt is enraged, approaches.

CAPULET   How now, kinsman, wherefore storm you so?

TYBALT   Uncle, this is a Montague, our foe!

CAPULET   Young Romeo, is it?

TYBALT   'Tis he, that villain Romeo.

CAPULET   Content thee, gentle coz, let him alone.

TYBALT   I'll not endure him!

CAPULET   He shall be endured! Go to, am I the master here or you? Go to, go to!

Old Capulet bustles away, leaving Tybalt to stare murderously towards Romeo. Romeo, unaware of the hostility he has aroused, has managed to obtain the unknown beauty as his partner in the dance. He takes her hand and holds up his mask.

ROMEO   If I profane with my unworthiest hand this holy shrine, the gentle sin is this, my lips, two blushing pilgrims, ready stand to smooth that rough touch with a tender kiss.

JULIET   Good pilgrim, you do wrong your hand too much, which mannerly devotion shows in this: saints have hands that pilgrims' hands do touch, and palm to palm is holy palmer's kiss.

ROMEO   Have not saints lips, and holy palmers too? (*Gently, and under the concealment of the mask, he kisses her.*) O trespass sweetly urged. Give me my sin again!

They kiss again.

JULIET   You kiss by th'book—

As they converse, lost in each other, Juliet's nurse, a busy, capacious dame approaches.

NURSE   —Madam— (*hastily, the lovers' faces fly apart*) —your mother craves a word with you.

Obediently, Juliet departs.

ROMEO   What is her mother?

NURSE   Marry, bachelor, her mother is the lady of the house. I nursed her daughter that you talked withal. I tell you— (*she winks and digs Romeo in the ribs*) —he that can lay hold of her shall have the chinks. (*She bustles away.*)

ROMEO   Is she a Capulet? O dear account. My life is my foe's debt!

Aghast at this blow of fortune, Romeo disappears among the dancers. Juliet, having done with her mother, returns.

JULIET   Come hither, Nurse. What's he that is now going out of door?

NURSE   I know not. (*She speaks evasively.*)

JULIET   Go ask his name. If he be married, my grave is like to be my wedding bed.

NURSE   His name is Romeo, and a Montague, the only son of your great enemy.

JULIET   My only love sprung from my only hate! Too early seen unknown, and known too late!

NURSE   What's this? What's this?

JULIET   A rhyme I learned even now, of one I danced withal.

NURSE   (*leading Juliet away*) Anon, anon! Come let's away, the strangers are all gone!

Night. The moon shines brightly on the orchard of the Capulets' house. There is a balcony, like a carved stone pocket, from which Juliet surveys the moonlight.

JULIET   O Romeo, Romeo, wherefore art thou Romeo? Deny thy father and refuse thy name . . . 'Tis but thy name that is my enemy; thou art thyself, though not a Montague. What's in a name? That which we call a rose by any other word would smell as sweet: so Romeo would, were he not Romeo called. Romeo, doff thy name, and for thy name, which is no part of thee, take all myself.

Suddenly, Romeo appears from the shadows and stands below the balcony.

ROMEO	I take thee at thy word! Call me but love and I'll be new baptised: henceforth I never will be Romeo!
JULIET	How cam'st thou hither? The orchard walls are high and hard to climb—
ROMEO	—With love's light wings—
JULIET	—And the place death, considering who thou art, if any of my kinsmen find thee here!
ROMEO	Thy kinsmen are no stop to me!
JULIET	If they do see thee, they will murder thee!
ROMEO	Alack, there lies more peril in thine eye than twenty of their swords! Look thou but sweet and I am proof against their enmity!

JULIET   Thou knowest the mask of night is on my face, else would a maiden blush bepaint my cheek for that which thou hast heard me speak tonight. Fain would I deny what I have spoke. But farewell, compliment. Dost thou love me? I know thou wilt say 'Ay', and I will take thy word. O gentle Romeo, if thou dost love, pronounce it faithfully—

ROMEO   Lady, by yonder blessed moon I vow—

JULIET   O swear not by the moon, the inconstant moon—

ROMEO   What shall I swear by?

JULIET   Do not swear at all.

ROMEO   If my heart's dear love—

JULIET   Well, do not swear. Although I joy in thee, I have no joy of this contract tonight: it is too rash, too unadvised, too sudden, too like the lightning, which doth cease to be ere one can say 'It lightens'. Sweet, good night.

ROMEO   O wilt thou leave me so unsatisfied?

JULIET   What satisfaction canst thou have tonight? I hear some noise within. Dear love, adieu.

NURSE'S VOICE   (*from within*) Madam.

JULIET   (*to Romeo*) Stay but a little, I will come again. (*She leaves the balcony for her room.*)

ROMEO   I am afeard, being in night, all this is but a dream.

Juliet returns.

JULIET Three words, dear Romeo, and good night indeed. If thy bent of love be honourable, thy purpose marriage, send me word tomorrow by one that I'll procure to come to thee, where and what time thou wilt perform the rite, and all my fortunes at thy foot I'll lay . . .

ROMEO How silver-sweet sound lovers' tongues by night . . .

JULIET What o'clock tomorrow shall I send to thee?

ROMEO By the hour of nine.

NURSE (*within*) Madam—

JULIET Anon, good Nurse! Good night, good night. Parting is such sweet sorrow that I shall say good night till it be morrow.

Morning. A busy street. Mercutio and Benvolio are seeking Romeo, calling out his name and shouting up at windows, to the annoyance of those within, most of all to the annoyance of the house of Rosalyne where they strongly suspect Romeo is concealed.

MERCUTIO Where the devil should this Romeo be? Came he not home tonight?

BENVOLIO Not to his father's; I spoke with his man. Tybalt, the kinsman to old Capulet, hath sent a letter to his father's house.

TYBALT A challenge, on my life!

BENVOLIO Romeo will answer it. Here comes Romeo!

Romeo enters, all dreamy softness and smiles.

MERCUTIO You gave us the counterfeit fairly last night.

ROMEO Good morrow to you both. What counterfeit did I give you?

MERCUTIO The slip, sir, the slip!

As they converse, the nurse appears, bustling along the street, preceded by her servant. She is a veritable galleon of a figure.

ROMEO	Here's goodly gear! A sail! A sail!
MERCUTIO	Two. Two. A shirt and a smock!

At once the three friends seize hold of the nurse and twirl her round and round. At length, the foolery subsides. The nurse is panting for breath.

NURSE	Out upon you! Gentlemen, can any of you tell me where I can find the young Romeo? (*Romeo bows in acknowledgement.*) If you be he, sir, I desire some confidence with you.
MERCUTIO	She will invite him to some supper.

Romeo waves his friends away. Mockingly, they bow as they depart.

MERCUTIO	Farewell, ancient lady, farewell . . .

NURSE   (*to Romeo*) Pray you, sir, a word—my young lady bid me enquire you out. What she bid me say, I will keep to myself. But first let me tell ye, if ye should lead her into a fool's paradise, as they say, it were a very gross behaviour, as they say; for the gentlewoman is young.

ROMEO   Nurse, commend me to thy lady and mistress. Bid her devise some means to come to shrift this afternoon, and there she shall at Friar Laurence's cell, be shrived and married.

NURSE   Now God in heaven bless thee. This afternoon, sir? Well, she shall be there.

In her apartment in the Capulets' house, Juliet waits impatiently for the return of the nurse, alternately pacing the floor and rushing to the window.

JULIET   The clock struck nine when I did send the Nurse, in half an hour she promised to return. Had she affections and warm youthful blood she would have been as swift in motion as a ball. But old folks, many feign as they were dead—unwieldy, slow, heavy, and pale as lead. O God she comes! (*She flies from the room to greet the nurse.*) O honey Nurse, what news? Hast thou met with him?

NURSE   Jesu, what haste. Can you not stay awhile? Do you not see I am out of breath?

JULIET   How art thou out of breath to say thou art out of breath? Is thy news good or bad?

NURSE   Lord, how my head aches—

JULIET   What says he of our marriage?

NURSE   O God's lady dear, are you so hot?

JULIET   Come, what says Romeo?

NURSE   Have you got leave to go to shrift today?

JULIET   I have.

NURSE   Then hie you hence to Friar Laurence' cell. There stays a husband to make you a wife.

Juliet stares at the nurse, then embraces her wildly.

Friar Laurence's cell. A plain, white-washed room with an altar and crucifix above. The window looks out upon a neat herb garden. Romeo is waiting, in company with the friar, a kindly old man in monkish habit.

FRIAR   So smile the heavens on this holy act that after-hours with sorrow chide us not.

ROMEO   (*impatiently*) Amen, amen. Do thou but close our hands with holy words, then love-devouring death do what he dare—

FRIAR   These violent delights have violent ends— (*he glances through the window*) Here comes the lady.

Juliet enters, as if blown in by the summer breeze. At once, she and Romeo embrace.

FRIAR   Come, come with me and we will make short work, for, by your leaves, you shall not stay alone till holy church incorporate two in one.

He leads them to the altar, where, side by side, they kneel before the friar.

A street, in blazing sunshine, making the shadows sharp as knives. Mercutio and Benvolio are together.

BENVOLIO   I pray thee, good Mercutio, let's retire; the day is hot, the Capel are abroad, and if we meet we shall not 'scape a brawl, for now, these hot days, is the mad blood stirring. (*Even as he speaks, Tybalt and his followers appear.*) By my head, here comes the Capulets!

MERCUTIO   By my heel, I care not.

TYBALT   Gentlemen, good e'en: a word with one of you. Mercutio, thou consortest with Romeo.

MERCUTIO   Consort? What, dost thou make us minstrels?

Mercutio's hand goes to his sword; but, at that moment, Romeo appears in the street. He walks as if on air. He is every inch the new-made bridegroom. He is holding a red rose, doubtless the late property of Juliet.

TYBALT   Peace be with you, sir, here comes my man. (*He addresses the rapturous Romeo.*) Boy, turn and draw. (*He flicks the flower from Romeo's hand with his rapier.*)

ROMEO   I do protest. I never injured thee, but love thee better than thou canst devise—

MERCUTIO   (*outraged*) O calm, dishonourable, vile submission! Tybalt, you ratcatcher! Will you walk?

TYBALT   I am for you! (*Tybalt and Mercutio begin to fight.*)

ROMEO   Gentlemen, for shame! Hold, Tybalt! Good Mercutio!

He tries to pull Mercutio away. Tybalt lunges with his rapier, and pierces Mercutio. Mercutio cries out and Tybalt stares, amazed, at his blood-stained blade.

The Capulets fly from the scene. Mercutio staggers. Romeo makes to support him. Mercutio pushes him away, angrily. He sinks to the ground.

MERCUTIO   I am hurt. A plague o' both your houses. I am sped. Is he gone and hath nothing?

ROMEO   What, art thou hurt?

MERCUTIO   Ay, ay, a scratch, a scratch. Marry, 'tis enough.

ROMEO   Courage, man, the hurt cannot be much.

MERCUTIO   No, 'tis not so deep as a well, nor so wide as a church door, but 'tis enough. Ask for me tomorrow and you shall find me a grave man. I am peppered, I warrant, for this world. A plague o' both your houses. Why the devil came you between us? I was hurt under your arm.

ROMEO   I thought all for the best.

MERCUTIO   A plague o' both your houses! They have made worm's meat of me . . .

Mercutio dies. As Romeo looks down, shamed by his friend's reproach and grief-stricken by his death, a shadow falls across the body of Mercutio. Romeo looks up. Tybalt has returned. Enraged, Romeo draws his sword. They fight. Tybalt is killed.

Romeo stares in horror at what he has done. A crowd begins to gather. Benvolio seizes Romeo by the arm.

BENVOLIO   Romeo, away, be gone! The Prince will doom thee to death!

ROMEO   O, I am fortune's fool!

Romeo flies for his life.

Night. Friar Laurence's cell. The door opens. The good friar enters, bearing a lantern that casts wild shadows.

FRIAR   Romeo, come forth, come forth, thou fearful man.

Romeo emerges palely from the shadows.

ROMEO   Father, what news? What is the Prince's doom?

FRIAR   A gentler judgement vanished from his lips: not body's death, but body's banishment. Hence from Verona art thou banished—

ROMEO   'Tis torture and not mercy! Heaven is here where Juliet lives, and every cat and dog and little mouse, every unworthy thing lives here in heaven and may look on her, but Romeo may not—

FRIAR   Thou fond mad man, hear me a little speak— (*There is a knocking on the door.*) Who's there?

NURSE'S VOICE   I come from Lady Juliet.

The nurse enters.

ROMEO   Nurse!

NURSE   Ah sir, ah sir, death's the end of all.

ROMEO   Spak'st thou of Juliet? How is it with her? Doth not she think me an old murderer now I have stained the childhood of our joy with blood removed but little from her own?

NURSE   O, she says nothing, sir, but weeps and weeps, and now falls on her bed, and then starts up, and Tybalt calls, and then on Romeo cries, and then down falls again.

Romeo draws his dagger as if to kill himself.

FRIAR   Hold thy desperate hand. Go, get thee to thy love as was decreed, ascend her chamber—hence, and comfort her. But look thou stay not till the Watch be set, for then thou canst not pass to Mantua where thou shalt live till we can find a time to blaze your marriage, reconcile your friends, beg pardon of the Prince and call thee back . . .

NURSE   Hie you, make haste, for it grows very late.

FRIAR   Go hence, good night: either be gone before the Watch is set, or by the break of day . . .

Juliet's balcony. The night is giving way to a ragged grey dawn. A lark begins to sing. Romeo comes out of the bedchamber onto the balcony. Juliet follows . . .

JULIET   Wilt thou be gone? It is not yet near day, it was the nightingale and not the lark—

ROMEO   It was the lark, the herald of the morn. Look, love, night's candles are burnt out, and jocund day stands tiptoe on the misty mountain tops. I must be gone and live, or stay and die.

JULIET	Yond light is not daylight, I know it—
ROMEO	Come death, and welcome. Juliet wills it so. It is not day—
JULIET	It is, it is. Hie hence, begone, away. It is the lark that sings so out of tune—
NURSE'S VOICE	Madam, your lady mother is coming to your chamber. The day is broke, be wary, look about.

Romeo and Juliet embrace passionately; then Romeo descends a rope ladder that hangs from the balcony.

ROMEO	Farewell, farewell.

Juliet stares down into the darkness in which Romeo's face gleams palely, like a drowned man.

JULIET	O think'st thou we shall ever meet again?
ROMEO	I doubt it not—
JULIET	O God, I have an ill-divining soul! Methinks I see thee, now thou art so low, as one dead in the bottom of a tomb.
ROMEO	Adieu, adieu!

With a last wave, he vanishes. Juliet stares vainly for another glimpse of him. Lady Capulet enters the bedchamber. Juliet hastily leaves the balcony and returns inside.

LADY CAPULET	Why, how now, Juliet?
JULIET	Madam, I am not well.
LADY CAPULET	Evermore weeping for your cousin's death? Well, well, thou hast a careful father, child; one who to put thee from heaviness hath sorted out a day of sudden joy—
JULIET	What day is that?
LADY CAPULET	Marry, my child, early next Thursday morn the gallant, young and noble gentleman, the County Paris, at Saint Peter's Church, shall happily make thee there a joyful bride!
JULIET	(*aghast*) Now by Saint Peter's Church, and Peter too, he shall not make me there a happy bride! I will not marry yet. And when I do, I swear it shall be Romeo, whom you know I hate, rather than Paris—
LADY CAPULET	Here comes your father, tell him so yourself.

CAPULET	How now, wife, have you delivered to her our decree?
LADY CAPULET	Ay sir, but she will have none.
CAPULET	How? Will she none? Does she not give us thanks? (*He turns, furiously, upon his daughter*) Mistress minion you, but fettle your fine joints 'gainst Thursday next to go with Paris to Saint Peter's Church, or I will drag thee on a hurdle thither. Out, you green-sickness carrion! Out, you baggage!

JULIET   (*kneeling*) Good father, I beseech you—

CAPULET   Hang thee, young baggage, disobedient wretch! I tell thee what—get thee to church a Thursday or never after look me in the face! (*He storms out, followed by Lady Capulet.*)

JULIET   O God!—O Nurse, comfort me, counsel me!

NURSE   I think it best you married with the County. O, he's a lovely gentleman. Romeo's a dishclout to him.

JULIET   (*drawing away from the nurse and staring at her bitterly*) Well, thou hast comforted me marvellous much. Go in, and tell my lady I am gone, having displeased my father, to Laurence' cell, to make confession and be absolved.

NURSE   Marry, I will, and this is wisely done. (*She departs.*)

JULIET   Ancient damnation! O most wicked fiend! Thou and my bosom shall henceforth be twain. I'll to the Friar to know his remedy; if all else fail, myself have power to die.

In Friar Laurence's cell. Juliet kneels before the friar.

JULIET   God joined my heart and Romeo's, thou our hands; and ere this hand, by thee to Romeo sealed, or my true heart with treacherous revolt turn to another, this shall slay them both. (*She takes a dagger from her bosom.*)

FRIAR   Hold, daughter. I do spy a kind of hope. Go home, be merry, give consent to marry Paris. Wednesday is tomorrow; tomorrow night look that thou lie alone. Let not the Nurse lie with thee in thy chamber. (*He takes a small bottle from a shelf and gives it to her.*) Take thou this vial, being then in bed, and this distilling liquor drink thou off . . . Now when the bridegroom in the morning comes to rouse thee from thy bed, there thou art, dead. Then as the manner of our country is, in thy best robes, thou shalt be borne to that same ancient vault where all the kindred of the Capulets lie. In this borrowed likeness of shrunk death thou shalt continue two and forty hours and then awake as from a pleasant sleep. In the meantime, against thou shalt awake, shall Romeo by my letters

know our drift and hither shall he come, and he and I will watch thy waking, and that very night shall Romeo bear thee hence to Mantua.

Juliet nods and, clutching the vial, departs. Hastily, Friar Laurence writes a letter and summons Friar John, a brother of his order, to take the letter to Romeo in Mantua.

A street in Mantua. Romeo waits, his eyes never leaving the road that leads to Verona. A horseman appears and rides towards him. It is his servant.

ROMEO   News from Verona! How doth my lady? Is my father well? How doth my Juliet? That I ask again, for nothing can be ill if she be well!

SERVANT	Then she is well and nothing can be ill. Her body sleeps in Capels' monument. I saw her laid low in her kindred's vault. O pardon me for bringing you these ill news.
ROMEO	Is it e'en so? (*The servant nods.*) Then I defy you, stars! I will hence tonight!
SERVANT	I do beseech you, sir, have patience!
ROMEO	Leave me. Hast thou no letters to me from the Friar?
SERVANT	None, my good lord.
ROMEO	No matter. Get thee gone. (*The servant leaves him.*) Well, Juliet, I will lie with thee tonight. Let's see for means. O mischief thou art swift to enter in the thoughts of desperate men. I do remember an apothecary . . .

The apothecary's shop. 'In his needy shop a tortoise hung, an alligator stuffed, and other skins of ill-shaped fishes; and about his shelves a beggarly account of empty boxes, green earthenware pots, bladders and musty seeds, remnants of packthread, and old cakes of roses . . .' Romeo enters, and the apothecary comes to attend him: 'in tattered weeds, with overwhelming brows.' Romeo leans upon the counter and beckons.

ROMEO   Come hither, man. I see thou art poor. There is forty ducats. Let me have a dram of poison.

APOTHECARY   Such mortal drugs I have, but Mantua's law is death to any he that utters them.

ROMEO   Art thou so bare and full of wretchedness, and fear'st to die? The world is not thy friend, nor the world's law; the world affords no law to make thee rich; then be not poor, but break it, and take this. (*He pushes the money across the counter.*)

APOTHECARY   (*staring at the money*) My poverty, but not my will consents.

ROMEO   I pay thy poverty and not thy will.

The apothecary fumbles on his shelves and takes down a vial, which he lays on the counter. The withered hand of the apothecary and the fine white hand of Romeo cross: one takes the gold, the other, the poison.

ROMEO   I sell thee poison, thou hast sold me none. Farewell, buy food, get thyself in flesh.

He hastens from the shop.

Friar Laurence's cell. Friar Laurence looks up from his studies as Friar John enters.

FRIAR LAURENCE   Friar John, welcome from Mantua. What says Romeo?

Friar John gravely shakes his head.

FRIAR JOHN   Going to find a barefoot brother out, one of our order, to associate me, here in this city visiting the sick, and finding him, the searchers of the town, suspecting that we both were in a house where the infectious pestilence did reign, sealed up the doors and would not let us forth, so that my speed to Mantua there was stayed.

FRIAR LAURENCE   Who bare my letter then to Romeo?

FRIAR JOHN   I could not send it—here it is again—

FRIAR LAURENCE   Unhappy fortune! Now must I to the monument alone! Within these three hours will the fair Juliet wake!

In the utmost agitation, he leaves the cell; then, a moment later, returns for his lantern. He rushes forth again, and Friar John, full of guilt, watches Friar Laurence, lit by his lantern, whirl off into the dark . . .

Within the monument of the Capulets. Juliet lies motionless on her bier, illuminated by four tall candles. About her, in the shadowy gloom, lie broken coffins on shelves . . . some with bones protruding and skulls peeping inquisitively forth, as if to welcome their fair new neighbour. Romeo enters. He approaches Juliet, and kneels beside her.

ROMEO   O my love, my wife! Death that hath sucked the honey of thy breath hath had no power upon thy beauty yet. Thou art not conquered. Beauty's ensign yet is crimson on thy lips and in thy cheeks, and Death's pale flag is not advanced there. Here, here will I remain with worms that are thy chambermaids; O here will I set up my everlasting rest . . . Eyes look your last! Arms take your last embrace! And lips, O you the doors of breath, seal with a righteous kiss a dateless bargain with engrossing Death!

He kisses Juliet, then holds up the vial of poison like a glass of wine.

ROMEO   Here's to my love! (*He drinks.*) O true Apothecary, thy drugs are quick!

He kisses Juliet again, then dies. A moment later, Friar Laurence enters the tomb. He gazes in despair at the scene. Slowly, Juliet stirs. She sees the friar.

JULIET   O comfortable Friar, where is my lord? (*She stares about her at the images of death and decay.*) I do remember well where I should be, and there I am. Where is my Romeo?

FRIAR   I hear some noise. Lady, come from that nest of death, contagion, and unnatural sleep. A greater power than we can contradict hath thwarted our intents. Come, come away! Thy husband in thy bosom there lies dead. Come, I'll dispose of thee among a sisterhood of holy nuns. Stay not to question, for the Watch is coming. Come, go, good Juliet. I dare no longer stay.

JULIET   (*with quiet dignity*) Go, get thee hence, for I will not away.

The friar, wringing his hands in grief and dismay, departs. Juliet rises, and kneels beside the dead Romeo. She takes his hand and discovers the vial, still clutched in it.

JULIET   What's here? A cup closed in my true love's hand? Poison, I see, hath been his timeless end. (*She takes it, and sees it to be empty.*) O churl. Drunk all, and left no friendly drop to help me after? I will kiss thy lips. Haply some poison yet doth hang on them. (*She kisses him.*) Thy lips are warm—

There are sounds of people approaching: shouts and cries as they approach the tomb.

JULIET   Yea, a noise? Then I'll be brief. (*She takes Romeo's dagger.*) O happy dagger. This is thy sheath. There rust, and let me die. (*She stabs herself and falls lifeless into the arms of the dead Romeo.*)

Figures come crowding into the tomb, flourishing torches. Among the awed faces are old Capulet and Montague. Then comes the Prince. He surveys the tragic scene, and turns to the bereaved parents.

PRINCE   Capulet, Montague, see what a scourge is laid upon your hate, that heaven finds means to kill your joys with love . . .

CAPULET   O brother Montague, give me thy hand. This is my daughter's jointure, for no more can I demand.

MONTAGUE   But I can give thee more, for I will raise her statue in pure gold, that whiles Verona by that name is known, there shall no figure at such rate be set as that of true and faithful Juliet.

CAPULET   As rich shall Romeo's by his lady lie, poor sacrifices to our enmity.

The curtain falls, not on the darkness of the lovers' tomb, but on the brightness of it.

HAMLET

The curtain rises on the battlements of a dark and forbidding castle. It is night. Three figures are huddled together. They are Marcellus and Barnardo, sentinels, and Horatio, a visitor to the castle. They are staring fearfully about them.

MARCELLUS   Look where it comes again!

Out of the swirling nothingness comes a ghostly figure, all in armour. Slowly it stalks by; and its face, seen beneath its helmet, is filled with gloom.

BARNARDO   In the same figure like the king that's dead!

MARCELLUS   Is it not like the king, Horatio?

HORATIO   As thou art to thyself. (*The apparition vanishes.*) Let us impart what we have seen unto young Hamlet.

They all stare after the vanished phantom.

MARCELLUS   Something is rotten in the state of Denmark.

In the royal council chamber, the king and queen sit fondly side by side. Behind them stands Polonius, the doting old Lord Chamberlain. The brightly coloured court looks smiling on. But one figure sits apart, and all in black. It is Prince Hamlet. He stares at his mother, the queen, then turns away.

HAMLET (*to himself*) That it should come to this! A little month, or ere those shoes were old with which she followed my poor father's body—O God, a beast that wants discourse of reason would have mourned longer!—married to my uncle, my father's brother, but no more like my father than I to Hercules!

As he murmurs to himself, a young man of the court comes and kneels before the king.

KING What wouldst thou beg, Laertes?

LAERTES My dread lord, your leave and favour to return to France.

KING Have you your father's leave? What says Polonius?

POLONIUS He hath, my lord, wrung from me my slow leave.

KING Take thy fair hour, Laertes. (*Laertes bows and withdraws.*) But now my cousin Hamlet, and my son—

HAMLET (*aside*) A little more than kin, and less than kind.

KING —how is it that the clouds still hang upon you?

QUEEN   Good Hamlet, cast thy nighted colour off. Do not for ever seek for thy noble father in the dust. Thou know'st 'tis common: all that lives must die.

HAMLET   Ay, madam, it is common.

QUEEN   If it be, why seems it so particular with thee?

HAMLET   Seems, madam? Nay, it is. I know not 'seems'.

KING   'Tis sweet and commendable in your nature, Hamlet, to give these mourning duties to your father, but you must know your father lost a father, that father lost, lost his.—We pray you, throw to earth this unprevailing woe . . .

Hamlet stares at him. The king sighs, and, with his queen, leaves the chamber, followed by the court.

HAMLET   Frailty, thy name is woman!

Enter Horatio, Barnardo and Marcellus. Hamlet smiles.

HAMLET   Horatio, or I do forget myself! But what is your affair in Elsinore?

HORATIO   My lord, I came to see your father's funeral.

HAMLET   I prithee, do not mock me, fellow-student. I think it was to see my mother's wedding.

HORATIO	Indeed, my lord, it followed hard upon.
HAMLET	Thrift, thrift, Horatio. The funeral baked meats did coldly furnish forth the marriage tables! (*He sighs and gazes into the distance.*) My father—methinks I see my father—
HORATIO	Where, my lord?
HAMLET	In my mind's eye, Horatio.
HORATIO	My lord, I think I saw him yesternight.
HAMLET	Saw? Who? For God's love let me hear!
HORATIO	Two nights together had these gentlemen on their watch been thus encountered. A figure like your father, armed at point exactly, appears before them, and with solemn march goes slow and stately by them. Thrice he walked. I knew your father, these hands are not more like.

HAMLET	But where was this?
MARCELLUS	My lord, upon the platform where we watched.
HAMLET	Stayed it long?
HORATIO	While one with moderate haste might tell a hundred.
MARCELLUS AND BARNARDO	(*shaking their heads*) Longer, longer!

HORATIO	Not when I saw it.
HAMLET	I will watch tonight, perchance 'twill walk again. Fare you well. (*Horatio and his companions withdraw.*) My father's spirit, in arms! All is not well!

A room in the castle. Laertes, prepared for France, is bidding farewell to Ophelia, his sister.

LAERTES	My necessaries are embarked, farewell. And sister, do not sleep but let me hear from you.
OPHELIA	Do you doubt that?
LAERTES	For Hamlet, and the trifling of his favour, hold it a fashion, and a toy in the blood, no more.
OPHELIA	No more but so?
LAERTES	Fear it, Ophelia, fear it, my dear sister, and keep you in the rear of his affection . . . But here my father comes!

Enter Polonius, full of bustle and importance.

POLONIUS	Yet here, Laertes? Aboard, aboard for shame! The wind sits in the shoulder of your sail, and you are stayed for! There, my blessing with thee!
LAERTES	Farewell, Ophelia, and remember well what I have said to you.
OPHELIA	'Tis in my memory locked.

LAERTES	Farewell. (*He embraces her, and departs.*)
POLONIUS	What is't, Ophelia, he hath said to you?
OPHELIA	So please you, something touching the Lord Hamlet.
POLONIUS	What is't between you? Give me up the truth.
OPHELIA	He hath, my lord, of late made many tenders of his affections to me.
POLONIUS	Affection? Pooh, you speak like a green girl!
OPHELIA	My lord, he hath importuned me with love in honourable fashion.
POLONIUS	Go to, go to! From this time be somewhat scanter of your maiden presence. I would not, in plain terms, from this time forth, have you so slander any moment leisure as to give words or talk with the Lord Hamlet. Look to it, I charge you!
OPHELIA	I shall obey you.

Night on the battlements. Hamlet, Horatio and Marcellus stand together.

HAMLET	What hour now?
HORATIO	I think it lacks of twelve.
MARCELLUS	No, it is struck.

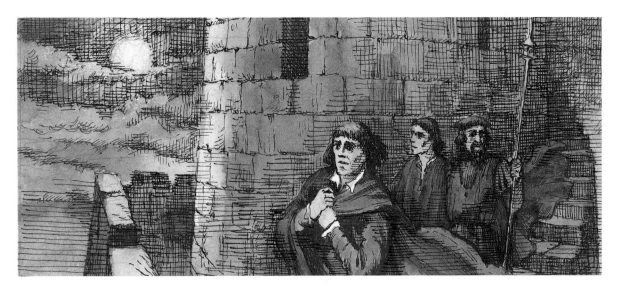

HORATIO   Indeed, I heard it not. It then draws near the season wherein the spirit held his wont to walk. (*They stare into the dark.*) Look, my lord, it comes!

The ghost appears, and stalks towards Hamlet.

HAMLET   Angels and ministers of grace defend us! (*The ghost beckons.*) I will follow it!

HORATIO   Do not, my lord!

HAMLET   Why, what should be the fear? I do not set my life at a pin's fee, and for my soul, what can it do to that, being a thing immortal as itself. I'll follow it!

MARCELLUS   You shall not, my lord!

HORATIO   Be ruled: you shall not go!

They try to restrain Hamlet. He frees himself and draws his sword.

HAMLET   By heaven, I'll make a ghost of him that lets me! I say away!

The ghost, ever beckoning to Hamlet, mounts steps towards a high, lonely platform. Hamlet follows.

HAMLET   Go on, I'll follow thee!

The platform is reached. Hamlet's companions have been left behind. Hamlet is alone with the ghost.

GHOST   I am thy father's spirit, doomed for a certain time to walk the night, and for the day confined to fast in fires, till the foul crimes done in my days of nature are burnt and purged away. (*Hamlet buries his face in his hands in horror.*) List, list, O list! If thou didst ever thy dear father love—

HAMLET   O God!

GHOST   Revenge his foul and most unnatural murder!

HAMLET   Murder!

GHOST   Murder most foul, as in the best it is. Now, Hamlet, hear. 'Tis given out that, sleeping in my orchard, a serpent stung me. But know thou, noble youth, the serpent that did sting thy father's life now wears his crown.

HAMLET   O my prophetic soul! My uncle!

GHOST   Ay, that incestuous, that adulterous beast, with witchcraft of his wit, with traitorous gifts, won to his shameful lust, the will of my most seeming virtuous queen. O Hamlet, what a falling-off was there! Let not the royal bed of Denmark be a couch for luxury and damned incest! But howsoever thou pursuest this act, taint not thy mind nor let thy soul contrive against thy mother aught. Leave her to Heaven . . . Fare thee well . . . Adieu, adieu, adieu. Remember me.

Little by little, the ghost fades into nothingness. Hamlet is left alone, weeping with grief, pity and rage.

HAMLET   Remember thee? Ay, thou poor ghost, whiles memory holds a seat in this distracted globe! (*He rushes to the edge of the platform and glares down towards the dark bulk of the castle, from which lights and faint sounds of revelry rise up.*) O most pernicious woman! O villain, villain, smiling damned villain! My tables! (*He drags out his student's commonplace book and begins to write in it feverishly.*) Meet it is I set it down that one may smile and smile and be a villain— so, uncle, there you are! Now to my word. It is, 'Adieu, adieu, remember me!' I have sworn it!
Voices call him from below: My lord, my lord! Lord Hamlet!

Hamlet descends from the platform, and greets his anxious, fearful companions.

MARCELLUS   How is't, my noble lord?

HORATIO   What news, Hamlet?

HAMLET   It is an honest ghost, that let me tell you. For your desire to know what is between us, o'ermaster it as you may. And now good friends, as you are friends, scholars and soldiers, give me one poor request.

HORATIO   What is't, my lord?

HAMLET   Never make known what you have seen tonight.

MARCELLUS AND HORATIO   My lord we will not.

HAMLET   Swear on my sword. (*He holds out his sword. Marcellus and Horatio lay their hands on it and swear. Hamlet now thrusts his sword at them again.*) Here as before, never, so help you mercy, how strange or odd so'er I bear myself, as I perchance hereafter shall think meet to put an antic disposition on, (*He falls into an attitude suggesting madness.*) to note that you know aught of me. Swear.

Much mystified, his companions swear again. Hamlet puts away his sword, and smiles at his friends.

HAMLET   Let us go in together. The time is out of joint, O cursed spite, that ever I was born to set it right.

*Hamlet skips ahead of his friends, turns, and adopts his
attitude of pretended madness. Then he lays a warning finger
to his lips, and shakes his head.*

*Polonius's apartment in the castle. Polonius is seated at a table.
Suddenly his daughter, Ophelia, comes rushing in. It is clear
that she is upset.*

OPHELIA	O my lord, my lord, I have been so affrighted!
POLONIUS	With what, i' the name of God?
OPHELIA	My lord, as I was sewing in my closet, Lord Hamlet, with his doublet all unbraced, pale as his shirt, his knees knocking each other, and with a look so piteous in purport as if he had been loosed out of hell to speak of horrors, he comes before me!
POLONIUS	Mad for thy love?
OPHELIA	My lord, I do not know, but truly I do fear it.
POLONIUS	(*rising and taking Ophelia firmly by the hand*) Come, go with me. I will go seek the king. This is the very ecstasy of love. (*He looks at her closely.*) Have you given him any hard words of late?
OPHELIA	No, my good lord, but as you did command, I did repel his letters and denied his access to me.
POLONIUS	That hath made him mad. Come, go we to the king.

In the royal apartment, the king and queen are seated, with courtiers in attendance. Polonius and Ophelia appear in the door. Then Polonius, examining the distraught looks of his daughter, decides she is unfit to be brought into the presence of the king. He sends her away and enters on his own.

POLONIUS (*triumphantly*) I have found the very cause of Hamlet's lunacy!

KING O speak of that: that do I long to hear!

QUEEN I doubt it is no other but the main: his father's death and our o'er-hasty marriage.

POLONIUS (*wisely shaking his head*) I will be brief. Your noble son is mad: mad call I it, for to define true madness, what is't but to be nothing else but mad? But let that go.

QUEEN (*impatiently*) More matter with less art.

POLONIUS Madam, I swear I use no art at all. That he's mad 'tis true, 'tis true 'tis pity, and pity 'tis 'tis true—a foolish figure, but farewell it, for I will use no art. Perpend. I have a daughter—have while she is mine—who in her duty and obedience, mark, hath given me this. (*He produces a letter which he reads.*) 'To the celestial, and my soul's idol, the most beautified Ophelia'—That's an ill phrase, a vile phrase, 'beautified' is a vile phrase. But you shall hear: 'O dear Ophelia, I am ill. I have not art to reckon my groans; but that I love thee best, O most best, believe it . . .'

QUEEN Came this from Hamlet to her?

Polonius nods and gives the queen the letter. She studies it and passes it to the king.

KING Do you think 'tis this?

QUEEN It may be; very like.

KING How may we try it further?

POLONIUS You know he walks sometimes four hours together here in the lobby? At such a time I'll loose my daughter to him. You and I, behind an arras there, mark the encounter.

KING We will try it.

Hamlet enters, his dress much disordered. He is reading a book.

QUEEN But look where sadly the poor wretch comes.

POLONIUS Away, I do beseech you both. I'll board him presently.

The king and queen, together with the courtiers, depart, leaving Polonius to confront Hamlet.

POLONIUS How does my good lord Hamlet?

HAMLET Well, God a-mercy.

POLONIUS Do you know me, my lord?

HAMLET	Excellent well. You are a fishmonger.
POLONIUS	Not I, my lord.
HAMLET	Then I would you were so honest a man.
POLONIUS	Honest, my lord?
HAMLET	Ay, sir, to be honest, as this world goes, is to be one man picked out of ten thousand.
POLONIUS	That's very true, my lord. (*Aside*) Though this be madness, yet there's method in't.
HAMLET	Have you a daughter?
POLONIUS	I have, my lord.
HAMLET	Let her not walk in the sun. Conception is a blessing, but as your daughter may conceive, friend, look to it.
POLONIUS	(*aside*) Still harping on my daughter. Yet he knew me not at first, he said I was a fishmonger. He is far gone. I'll speak to him again. Will you walk out of the air, my lord?
HAMLET	Into my grave.
POLONIUS	Indeed, that's out of the air. (*Aside*) How pregnant sometimes his replies are! (*To Hamlet*) My lord, I will take my leave of you.

HAMLET	You cannot, sir, take from me anything that I will more willingly part withal—except my life, except my life, except my life. (*Polonius bows and withdraws. Hamlet stares contemptuously after him.*) These tedious old fools!

He goes to a window and gazes out. Far below a cart toils up the hill towards the castle. It bears a huge banner on which is written: 'The best actors in the world, either for Comedy, Tragedy, History . . .' In the cart sit the actors themselves, a perfect painted court, not unlike the royal court of Denmark. Hamlet turns away.

HAMLET   (*thoughtfully*) I have heard that guilty creatures sitting at a play, have, by the very cunning of the scene, been struck so to the soul that presently they have proclaimed their malefactions! I will have these players play something like the murder of my father before mine uncle. I'll observe his looks. The spirit that I have seen may be a devil—and the devil hath power t'assume a pleasing shape. I'll have grounds more relative than this. The play's the thing wherein I'll catch the conscience of the king!

A lobby in the castle. The king and Polonius together.

They hide in an alcove behind a curtain. Enter Hamlet, reading. He looks up, deeply troubled.

HAMLET   To be, or not to be, that is the question: whether 'tis nobler in the mind to suffer the slings and arrows of outrageous fortune, or to take arms against a sea of troubles, and by opposing, end them. To die, to sleep—no more; and by a sleep to say we end the heartache and the thousand natural shocks that flesh is heir to; 'tis a consummation devoutly to be wished. To die, to sleep—to sleep, perchance to dream—ay, there's the rub, for in that sleep of death what dreams may come, when we have shuffled off this mortal coil, must give us pause . . .

Ophelia approaches.

OPHELIA   Good my lord, how does your honour for this many a day?

HAMLET   I humbly thank you, well, well, well.

OPHELIA   My lord, I have remembrances of yours that I have longed to redeliver. (*She approaches and holds out a bundle of ribbon-tied letters and a necklace.*) Rich gifts wax poor when givers prove unkind. There, my lord.

HAMLET   (*taking the offerings*) I did love you once.

OPHELIA   Indeed, my lord, you made me believe so.

HAMLET   You should not have believed me. I loved you not.

OPHELIA   I was the more deceived.

HAMLET   Get thee to a nunnery. Why, would'st thou be a breeder of sinners? Go thy ways to a nunnery! Where's your father?

OPHELIA   At home, my lord.

HAMLET   Let the doors be shut upon him, that he may play the fool nowhere but in's own house. To a nunnery go, and quickly too! Or if thou wilt needs marry, marry a fool. For wise men know well enough what monsters you make of them.

OPHELIA   Heavenly powers restore him!

HAMLET   I have heard of your paintings well enough. God hath given you one face, and you make yourselves another. You jig and amble, and you lisp, you nickname God's creatures and you make your wantonness your ignorance. Go to, I'll no more on't, it hath made me mad. I say we will have no more marriage. Those that are married already (all but one) shall live, the rest shall keep as they are. To a nunnery, go.

Hamlet flings the keepsakes in the air. Ophelia sinks to the ground. The king and Polonius emerge from concealment.

KING   Love? His affections do not that way tend. There's something in his soul . . . He shall with speed to England. Madness in great ones must not unwatched go.

The Court are all assembled in a great chamber, awaiting the performance of the players. A curtain hides the stage. The king and queen are sitting side by side. Hamlet sits beside Ophelia, and closely observes the king. The king beckons to Hamlet.

KING   Have you heard the argument? Is there no offence in't?

HAMLET   No, no, they do but jest—poison in jest. No offence i'the world!

The king nods. He signs to the musicians. They sound a fanfare. The curtain parts and reveals a painted orchard. The action of the play is carried on in dumbshow, to the accompaniment of music. The Player King and Player Queen come on, and fondly embrace.

The Player King lies down to sleep. The Player Queen draws aside. A murderer enters and cunningly pours poison in the Player King's sleeping ear. The Player King jerks in violent pain; then dies. The Player Queen rushes forward and clasps her dead husband with extravagant grief.

HAMLET   (*to the queen*) Madam, how like you this play?

QUEEN   The lady doth protest too much, methinks.

On the stage, the murderer takes the Player Queen by the arm, and offers her jewels. At first she resists, but then, little by little, she capitulates. The Player Queen and the murderer embrace passionately.

The king rises from his seat. He is enraged and terrified by the image of his own crime. The court rises in consternation.

HAMLET	What, frighted with false fire?
KING	Give me some light! Away!

He rushes away, followed by the distracted queen and all the court. Hamlet and Horatio are left alone.

HAMLET	O good Horatio, I'll take the ghost's word for a thousand pound. Didst perceive?
HORATIO	Very well, my lord!

Polonius returns, much agitated.

POLONIUS	My lord, the queen would speak with you.
HAMLET	I will come to my mother by and by. (*Aside*) I will speak daggers to her but use none.

In the queen's bedchamber. Polonius attempts to give counsel to the queen.

POLONIUS	Look you lay home to him, tell him his pranks have been too broad to bear with. Pray you be round!
QUEEN	Fear me not. Withdraw, I hear him coming!

Hastily, Polonius conceals himself behind a curtain. Hamlet enters, wild of aspect.

HAMLET   How now, mother, what's the matter?

QUEEN   Hamlet, thou hast thy father much offended.

HAMLET   Mother, you have my father much offended.

QUEEN   Come, come, you answer with an idle tongue.

HAMLET   Go, go, you question with a wicked tongue.

He stares at her menacingly. She retreats. He seizes her and forces her to sit on the bed.

HAMLET   Come, come, you shall not budge—

QUEEN   What wilt thou do? Thou wilt not murder me? Help, ho!

POLONIUS   *(behind the curtain)* What ho! Help!

HAMLET   *(rushing to the curtain)* How now? A rat! Dead for a ducat, dead! (*He thrusts his sword through the curtain. There is a cry, and the sound of a body falling. Hamlet draws out his bloody sword. He looks to the queen.*) Is it the King? (*He draws aside the curtain, and sees Polonius, dead.*)

QUEEN   O what a rash and bloody deed is this!

HAMLET   (*to the dead Polonius*) Thou wretched, rash, intruding fool, farewell; I took thee for thy better. Thou find'st to be too busy is some danger. (*To the queen*) Leave wringing your hands. Peace, sit you down, and let me wring your heart. (*They sit, side by side, on the bed. Hamlet holds up a locket he wears round his neck and shows it to his mother.*) Look here upon this picture, (*He drags a locket from his mother's neck and compares it with the other.*) and on this, the counterfeit presentment of two brothers. Have you eyes? Could you on this fair mountain feed and batten on this moor? Ha, have you eyes? You cannot call it love, for at your age the heyday in the blood is tame, it's humble and waits upon the judgement, and what judgement would step from this to this?

QUEEN	O speak to me no more. These words like daggers enter in my ears!
HAMLET	A murderer and a villain—
QUEEN	No more!
HAMLET	A king of shreds and patches—

Suddenly, the ghost appears. Hamlet stares at it, wild-eyed.

QUEEN	Alas, he's mad!
HAMLET	(*to ghost*) Do you not come your tardy son to chide?
GHOST	Do not forget. This visitation is to whet thy almost blunted purpose. But look, amazement on thy mother sits. Speak to her, Hamlet.
HAMLET	How is't with you, lady?
QUEEN	Alas, how is't with you? Whereon do you look?
HAMLET	On him, on him! Look you how pale he glares! Do you see nothing there?
QUEEN	Nothing at all—
HAMLET	Nor did you nothing hear?
QUEEN	No, nothing but ourselves!

The ghost begins to depart . . .

HAMLET   Why, look you there, look how it steals away, my father in his
          habit as he lived! Look where he goes!

QUEEN   This is the very coinage of your brain . . .

          *Hamlet shakes his head. He rises and goes to the dead
          Polonius.*

HAMLET   This man shall send me packing. I'll lug the guts into the
          neighbour room. This counsellor is now most still, most secret,
          and most grave, who was in life a foolish prating knave. (*He
          seizes hold of the dead man's feet and begins to drag him to the
          door.*) Come, sir, draw toward an end with you. Good night,
          mother.

          *Hamlet departs with the body. The king enters, followed by his
          attendants.*

KING   How does Hamlet?

QUEEN   Mad as the sea and wind. In his lawless fit, behind the arras
          hearing something stir, whips out his rapier, cries 'A rat, a rat!'
          and kills the unseen good old man!

KING   O heavy deed! Where is he gone?

QUEEN   To draw apart the body—

KING   (*to attendants*) Go seek him out!

The body of Polonius has not been found; but Hamlet has been seized and brought before the king.

KING   Now, Hamlet, where's Polonius?

HAMLET   At supper.

KING   At supper? Where?

HAMLET   Not where he eats, but where he's eaten; a certain convocation of politic worms are e'en at him.

KING   Where is Polonius?

HAMLET   In heaven, send thither to see; if your messenger find him not there, seek him i' the other place yourself. But if indeed you find him not within this month, you shall nose him as you go up the stairs into the lobby.

KING   (*to attendants*)Go seek him there. (*To Hamlet*) Hamlet, this deed must send thee hence. Therefore prepare thyself for England. (*Hamlet shrugs his shoulders and departs. The king looks after him savagely.*) England, if my love thou holds at aught, thou mayst not coldly set our sovereign process, which imports at full, by letters congruing to that effect, the present death of Hamlet! Do it, England, for like the hectic in my blood he rages, and thou must cure me!

In the royal apartment, the king and queen look to one another in dismay as a strange, distracted wailing is heard. Ophelia enters, all in ragged white, crying and laughing and singing. Wild flowers are in her hair, and she carries a posy. The death of her father and the loss of Hamlet have driven her mad.

OPHELIA (*singing*)   He is dead and gone, lady,
                         He is dead and gone . . .   (*She drifts away.*)

KING   O Gertrude, Gertrude, when sorrows come, they come not single spies, but in battalions . . .

There is a violent commotion outside. A soldier enters.

SOLDIER Save yourself, my lord! Young Laertes in riotous head o'erbears your officers! The rabble call him lord!

Laertes with armed followers, bursts in.

LAERTES (*to followers*) Sirs, stand you all without! O thou vile king, give me my father!

QUEEN   Calmly, good Laertes. (*She tries to restrain him.*)

KING   Let him go, Gertrude, do not fear our person. There's such divinity doth hedge a king that treason can but peep at what it would. Tell me, Laertes, why thou art thus incensed?

LAERTES   Where is my father?

KING   Dead.

QUEEN   But not by him!

KING   I am guiltless of thy father's death, and am—

He breaks off as a sound of strange singing is heard.

LAERTES   What noise is that?

Ophelia returns, in her distracted state. Laertes stares at her in horror.

OPHELIA   They bore him bare-faced on the bier
                   And on his grave rained many a tear—

She stops, and, plucking flowers from her posy, presents them to Laertes.

OPHELIA   There's rosemary, that's for remembrance. (*To the queen*) There's fennel for you, and columbines. (*To the king*) There's rue for you. And here's some for me. We may call it herb o' grace on Sundays. You must wear your rue with a difference. I would give you some violets, but they withered all when my father died. They say he made a good end.

All watch her, filled with pity. Laertes weeps for his sister.

OPHELIA   (*singing*)

> And will he not come again,
> And will he not come again?
> No, no, he's dead,
> Go to thy deathbed,
> He never will come again.

She drifts out of the apartment, out of the castle and into the woods beyond, until she comes to a stream, and there, still singing, clambers onto the branch of a willow, which breaks and casts her into the brook. 'Her clothes spread wide, and mermaid-like awhile they bore her up. But long it could not be till that her garments, heavy with their drink, pulled the poor wretch from her melodious lay to muddy death.'

The ship taking Hamlet to England has been attacked by pirates; and Hamlet, discovering the plot against his life, has boarded the pirate vessel and, in exchange for promises of reward, has been landed safely once more on Danish soil. He and Horatio are together, near to a churchyard. As they approach, they see a gravedigger at work, and singing.

GRAVEDIGGER

> In youth when I did love, did love,
> Methought it was very sweet . . .

HAMLET   Hath this fellow no feeling for his business? He sings in grave-making. (*He addresses the grave-digger*) What man dost thou dig for?

GRAVEDIGGER	For no man, sir.
HAMLET	For what woman then?
GRAVEDIGGER	For none neither.
HAMLET	Who is to be buried in it?
GRAVEDIGGER	One that was a woman, sir; but rest her soul, she's dead. (*He picks up a skull from the earth.*) Here's a skull now hath lien you i' the earth three-and-twenty years.
HAMLET	Whose was it?
GRAVEDIGGER	A whoreson mad fellow's it was! This same skull, sir, was Yorick's skull, the King's jester.

Hamlet takes the skull and gazes at it wonderingly.

HAMLET	This?
GRAVEDIGGER	E'en that.
HAMLET	Alas, poor Yorick, I knew him, Horatio, a fellow of infinite jest. (*To the skull*) No one now to mock your own grinning? Now get you to my lady's chamber, and tell her, let her paint an inch thick, to this favour she must come. Let her laugh at that. But soft, here comes the King, the Queen, the courtiers!

A funeral procession approaches. The king, queen, Laertes, and all the court follow a coffin. A priest is in attendance. Hamlet and Horatio withdraw behind a monument, to watch. The procession reaches the grave, and the coffin is lowered in. The priest turns away.

LAERTES   Must there be no more done? (*The priest shakes his head.*) I tell thee, churlish priest, a ministering angel shall my sister be when thou liest howling!

HAMLET   What, the fair Ophelia!

QUEEN   (*scattering flowers on the coffin*) Sweets to the sweet. Farewell.

LAERTES   Hold off the earth awhile, till I have caught her once more in mine arms!

He leaps down into the grave. Hamlet rushes upon the scene.

HAMLET   What is he whose grief bears such an emphasis?

LAERTES   (*looking up*) The devil take thy soul!

Hamlet leaps down into the grave and grapples with Laertes.

KING   Pluck them asunder!

QUEEN   Hamlet, Hamlet!

HAMLET I loved Ophelia! Forty thousand brothers could not with all their quantity of love make up my sum!

KING   O he is mad, Laertes!

QUEEN   For love of God, forbear him!

Courtiers drag the warring youths apart. They glare at each other. Then Hamlet shrugs his shoulders.

HAMLET Hear you, sir, what is the reason you use me thus? I loved you ever—but it is no matter. Let Hercules himself do what he may, the cat will mew, and dog will have his day.

An apartment in the castle. The king and Laertes are together.

KING   Hamlet comes back; what would you undertake in deed to show yourself your father's son?

LAERTES To cut his throat i' the church.

KING   (*nodding*) Will you be ruled by me?

LAERTES   Ay, my lord.

KING   You have been talked of since your travel much, and that in Hamlet's hearing, for a quality wherein they say you shine.

LAERTES   What part is that?

KING   For art and exercise in your defence, and for your rapier most especial. This report did Hamlet so envenom with his envy that he could do nothing but wish and beg your sudden coming o'er to play with you.

LAERTES   What out of this, my lord?

KING   Bring you in fine together, and wager on your heads. He being remiss, and free from all contriving, will not peruse the foils, so that with ease, or with a little shuffling, you may choose a sword unbated, and in a pass of practice requite him for your father!

LAERTES   (*eagerly*) I will do't, and for that purpose I'll anoint my sword. I bought an unction from a mountebank, so mortal that but to dip a knife in it . . . (*He makes an expressive gesture, indicating sudden death.*)

KING   Let's think further of this. When in your motion you are hot and dry, as make your bouts more violent to that end, and that he calls for drink, I'll have prepared him a chalice for the nonce, whereon but sipping, if he by chance escape your venomed stuck, our purpose may hold there.

They gaze into one another's eyes, deeply.

HAMLET

The great hall of the castle. Hamlet and Horatio are together. The fencing match with Laertes has been agreed to. A courtier enters.

COURTIER   My lord, his majesty sends to know if your pleasure hold to play with Laertes.

HAMLET   I am constant to my purpose. (*The courtier bows and departs.*)

HORATIO   You will lose, my lord.

HAMLET   I do not think so. But thou would'st not think how ill all's here about my heart—but no matter.

HORATIO   If your mind dislike anything, obey it. I will forestall their repair hither and say you are not fit.

HAMLET   We defy augury. There is special providence in the fall of a sparrow. The readiness is all. Let be.

Trumpets sound, heralding the approach of the king and queen, and all the court, to witness the fencing-match. They seat themselves. Foils are brought forward. They are offered first to Laertes. He chooses one, and flourishes it.

LAERTES   This is too heavy. Let me see another.

He takes another, which suits him better. He exchanges a secret nod with the king while Hamlet chooses a sword for himself.

HAMLET   This likes me well.

A servant brings a goblet of wine and sets it beside the king.

KING   Come, begin. And you, the judges, bear a wary eye.

The adversaries' swords are put together.

HAMLET   Come on, sir!

They fence. Hamlet scores a hit.

JUDGE   A hit, a very palpable hit!

The duellists part. The king frowns. He drops something in the goblet.

KING   Hamlet, this pearl is thine! Give him the cup!

HAMLET   I'll play this bout first. Set it by awhile. Come. (*They fence again. Again Hamlet scores a hit.*) Another hit, what say you?

LAERTES   I do confess't.

KING   (*to queen*) Our son shall win.

QUEEN   Here, Hamlet, take my napkin, rub thy brows. (*She takes up the goblet.*) The Queen carouses to thy fortune, Hamlet!

KING   Gertrude, do not drink!

QUEEN   I will, my lord, I pray you pardon me. (*She drinks.*)

KING   (*aside*) It is the poisoned cup! It is too late.

QUEEN   (*to Hamlet*) Come, let me wipe your face.

Hamlet goes to his mother, Laertes lunges at him and wounds his arm. Hamlet turns, incensed. They begin to fence again, but with a deadly fury. Suddenly Laertes is disarmed. Hamlet takes up the fallen sword, stares at its unbated tip. He throws his own sword to Laertes, and with the poisoned weapon begins to fight again. Laertes is wounded.

SERVANT   Look to the Queen!

The fighting stops. The queen has fallen back. She is dying.

KING   She swoons to see them bleed!

QUEEN   No, no, the drink, the drink! O my dear Hamlet! The drink, the drink! I am poisoned! (*She dies.*)

HAMLET   O villainy! Let the door be locked! Treachery, seek it out!

He rushes at the king. The court seeks to fly from the scene. Laertes has fallen. His wound is bleeding.

LAERTES   It is here, Hamlet. Hamlet, thou art slain, no medicine in the world can do thee good, in thee there is not half an hour of life. The treacherous instrument is in thine hand, unbated and envenomed. The foul practice hath turned itself on me. The King—the King's to blame!

Hamlet seizes the king and stabs him with the poisoned blade.

HAMLET   Venom, do thy work! (*He takes hold of the poisoned goblet and forces its contents down the king's throat.*) Here, thou incestuous, murderous, damned Dane, drink off this potion! Follow my mother! (*The king dies.*)

LAERTES   Exchange forgiveness with me, noble Hamlet.

Hamlet takes his offered hand. Then Laertes, doomed like all who had touched the corruption of the state, dies.

HAMLET   Heaven make thee free of it. I follow thee. (*He staggers. Horatio comes to support him.*) I am dead, Horatio. (*He tries to embrace the dead queen.*) Wretched Queen, adieu. (*He almost falls, and Horatio eases him into the chair from which the king has fallen.*) This fell sergeant, Death, is strict in his arrest. If thou didst ever hold me in thy heart, absent thee from felicity awhile, and in this harsh world draw thy breath in pain to tell my story . . . (*He tries to smile.*) The rest is silence . . . (*He dies.*)

HORATIO   Now cracks a noble heart. Good night, sweet prince, and flights of angels sing thee to thy rest.

The curtain falls . . .

TWELFTH NIGHT

The curtain rises on a wild sea upon which a fragile vessel is being tossed to and fro. Tremendous waves pound its sides as if to smash it like an egg-shell; and tiny figures fling themselves over the sides and strike out desperately for land.

Beyond its wild sea coast, Illyria is a green and pleasant land, ruled over by the Duke Orsino, a gentleman made melancholy by unrequited love . . .

In the Duke's mansion, he sits, listening to the sad music of a lute-player. Presently the music ceases.

DUKE   If music be the food of love, play on, give me excess of it . . .

As the lute-player resumes, the duke rises and goes to a window and gazes out towards a distant mansion. He sighs, for within that mansion is his love. She is the Countess Olivia, and she will have nothing to do with him.

In Olivia's house, all is sober and hung with black, for she is in mourning for a dead brother and has vowed to admit no thoughts of love for seven long years. But though all is mournful above stairs, in the wine cellar, like a stormy stomach below a calm face, riot ferments and bubbles in the person of her boozy uncle, Sir Toby Belch. He is with Maria, the countess's pretty waiting-woman.

SIR TOBY   What a plague means my niece to take the death of her brother thus? I am sure care's an enemy to life.

MARIA   By my troth, Sir Toby, you must come in earlier a'nights. Your cousin, my lady, takes great exception to your ill hours.

SIR TOBY   Why, let her except before excepted. (*He drinks.*)

MARIA   That quaffing and drinking will undo you: I heard my lady talk of it yesterday; and of a foolish knight that you brought in one night to be her wooer.

SIR TOBY   Who, Sir Andrew Aguecheek?

MARIA   Ay, he.

SIR TOBY   He's as tall as any man in Illyria!

MARIA   What's that to th'purpose?

SIR TOBY   Why, he has three thousand ducats a year.

MARIA	He's a very fool and a prodigal. He's drunk nightly in your company!
SIR TOBY	With drinking healths to my niece! I'll drink to her as long as there is a passage in my throat, and drink in Illyria! Here comes Sir Andrew Agueface!

Enter Sir Andrew Aguecheek, a tall, thin, fair-haired gentleman. He bows gallantly to Maria.

SIR ANDREW	Bless you, fair shrew!
MARIA	And you too, sir.
SIR ANDREW	Shall we not set about some revels?
SIR TOBY	What else shall we do? (*Gives Sir Andrew a drink.*) Let me see thee caper! (*Sir Andrew drinks and begins to dance, somewhat wildly.*) Ha, higher, higher!

Sir Toby joins in the dance and the two gentlemen clutch at Maria, who, helpless with laughter, evades them and makes her escape.

The sea-shore. A storm-battered boat lies on the beach and, beside it, some half dozen survivors from the shipwreck: among them is a young woman, Viola.

VIOLA   What country, friends, is this?

CAPTAIN   This is Illyria, lady.

VIOLA   And what should I do in Illyria? My brother, he is in Elysium. (*She gazes sadly out to sea.*) Perchance he is not drowned: what think you, sailors?

CAPTAIN   It is perchance that you yourself were saved.

VIOLA   O my poor brother! and so perchance may he be!

CAPTAIN   True, madam, and to comfort you with chance, assure yourself—After our ship did split, I saw your brother bind himself to a strong mast that lived upon the sea. I saw him hold acquaintance with the waves so long as I could see.

VIOLA   For saying so, there's gold! Knowest thou this country?

CAPTAIN   Ay, madam.

VIOLA   Who governs here?

CAPTAIN   Orsino.

VIOLA   Orsino! I have heard my father name him. I'll serve this duke. Thou shalt present me as an eunuch to him . . .

The captain nods, and Viola clasps him gratefully by the hand.

So Viola, with the captain's help, becomes Cesario, a page, and attired as a man, serves the duke in his palace.

COURTIER   If the duke continues these favours towards you, Cesario, you
            are like to be much advanced; he hath known you but three
            days and already you are no stranger.

            *The duke enters. Viola gazes at him, and it is evident that her
            feelings towards him are somewhat stronger than those of a
            page for his master.*

DUKE   Cesario, thou knowest no less but all: I have unclasped to thee
            the book even of my secret soul. (*He goes to the window and
            gazes towards the mansion of Olivia.*) Therefore, good youth,
            address thy gait unto her, be not denied access, stand at her
            doors, and tell them, there thy fixed foot shall grow till thou
            have audience.

VIOLA   Say I do speak with her, my lord, what then?

DUKE   O then unfold the passion of my love.

VIOLA   I'll do my best to woo your lady. (*She takes her departure,
            glancing back at the lovesick duke.*) Yet . . . whoe'er I woo,
            myself would be his wife!

            As Viola departs, the duke signs to his lute-player, who sings:

LUTE-PLAYER   Come away, come away death,
                        And in sad cypress let me be laid.
                        Fly away, fly away breath,
                        I am slain by a fair cruel maid . . .

The fair cruel maid is Olivia in her mansion, all in black. She is attended by solemn servants, and Feste, her jester, who tries, vainly, to make her smile.

OLIVIA   Take the fool away.

FESTE   Do you not hear, fellows? Take away the lady.

OLIVIA   Sir, I bade them take away you.

FESTE   Misprision in the highest degree! Good madonna, give me leave to prove you a fool.

OLIVIA   Can you do it?

FESTE   Dexteriously, madam. Good madonna, why mourn'st thou?

OLIVIA   Good fool, for my brother's death.

FESTE   I think his soul is in hell, madonna.

OLIVIA   I know his soul is in heaven, fool.

FESTE   The more fool, madonna, to mourn for your brother's soul, being in heaven. Take away the fool, gentlemen!

Maria enters with Olivia's steward, Malvolio, a solemn, long-faced personage, who looks exceedingly disapprovingly at the jester.

MARIA   Madam, there is at the gate a young gentleman much desires to speak with you.

OLIVIA   Tell him he shall not speak with me.

MALVOLIO   He has been told so; and says he'll stand at your door like a sheriff's post . . .

OLIVIA   What manner of man?

MALVOLIO   Of very ill manner: he'll speak with you, will you or no.

OLIVIA   Of what personage and years is he?

MALVOLIO   Not yet old enough for a man, nor young enough for a boy; as a squash is before 'tis a peascod. 'Tis with him in standing water, between boy and man.

OLIVIA   (*wearily*) Let him approach. (*Malvolio departs. Olivia turns to her maid, Maria.*) Give me my veil: come, throw it o'er my face. We'll once more hear Orsino's embassy.

Maria veils her mistress's face, and, with other black-gowned ladies of Olivia's court, stands behind her. Viola enters with a gallant flourish of her plumed cap. She is every inch the gentleman, and, one might say, with inches over and to spare.

VIOLA   The honourable lady of the house, which is she?

OLIVIA   Speak to me. I shall answer for her.

VIOLA   Most radiant, exquisite and unmatchable beauty—I pray you, tell me if this be the lady of the house, for I never saw her. I would be loath to cast away my speech. Are you the lady of the house?

OLIVIA   I am. Speak your office.

VIOLA   It alone concerns your ear.

Olivia gazes at the 'young man' thoughtfully.

OLIVIA   Give us this place alone. (*The attendants depart.*) Now sir, what is your text?

VIOLA   In Orsino's bosom.

OLIVIA   O, I have read it: it is heresy. Have you no more to say?

Viola stares curiously at the veiled face before her.

VIOLA   Good madam, let me see your face.

OLIVIA   Have you any commission from your lord to negotiate with my face? You are now out of your text; but we will draw the curtain, and show you the picture. (*She draws aside her veil.*) Is't not well done?

VIOLA   Excellently done, if God did all.

OLIVIA   'Tis in grain, sir, 'twill endure wind and weather.

VIOLA   'Tis beauty truly blent. Lady, you are the cruell'st she alive if you would lead these graces to the grave and leave the world no copy. My lord and master loves you. If I did love you in my master's flame, in your denial I would find no sense; I would not understand it.

OLIVIA   Why, what would you?

VIOLA   Make me a willow cabin at your gate, and call upon my soul within the house; write loyal cantons of contemnèd love, and sing them loud even in the dead of night; halloo your name to the reverberate hills, and make the babbling gossip of the air cry out 'Olivia!' O, you should not rest between the elements of earth and air but you should pity me!

OLIVIA   You might do much. What is your parentage?

VIOLA   Above my fortunes.

OLIVIA   Get you to your lord: I cannot love him: let him send no more, unless, perchance, you come to me again . . .

VIOLA   (*bowing her way out*) Farewell, fair cruelty!

Olivia gazes after the departed 'young man'. She sighs, and her eyes are filled with a sudden tenderness.

OLIVIA   What is your parentage? Above my fortunes. (*She sighs again.*) Malvolio!

The gloomy steward enters. Olivia beckons him close and murmurs to him.

Viola, her embassy completed as unsuccessfully as she could have wished, strides along the road towards the duke's palace. But she is being followed. Malvolio, his black coat flapping and his skinny black legs twinkling, hastens to overtake her.

MALVOLIO   Were you not even now with the Countess Olivia?

VIOLA   Even now, sir.

MALVOLIO   She returns this ring to you, sir. (*Disdainfully he holds out a ring to her. Viola stares at it, bewildered. Malvolio shrugs his shoulders, and drops it on the ground.*) If it be worth stooping for, there it lies: if not, be it his that finds it. (*He stalks away. Viola picks up the ring.*)

VIOLA   I left no ring with her: what means this lady? (*She is suddenly alarmed.*) She loves me, sure! Poor lady, she were better love a dream!

In the wine-cellar of the Countess's house, Feste, her fool, is singing to Sir Toby and Sir Andrew, while round about, like music-charmed monsters, great barrels and bottles wink and sway in the candlelight.

FESTE   O mistress mine, where are you roaming?
O stay and hear, your true love's coming,
That can sing both high and low.
Trip no further, pretty sweeting;
Journeys end in lovers meeting,
Every wise man's son doth know . . .

SIR ANDREW   A mellifluous voice, as I am a true knight.

SIR TOBY   But shall we make the welkin dance indeed?

SIR ANDREW   Let's do it! Come, begin!

They begin to sing a round, with much banging of tankards on the table. Maria enters, in her night attire.

MARIA   What a caterwauling do you keep here! (*Sir Toby catches her round the waist and, despite her protests, whirls her off in a drunken dance. The uproar continues. Malvolio enters, grim as death at a wedding.*)

MALVOLIO   My masters, are you mad? Have you no wit, manners nor honesty but to gabble like tinkers at this time of night?

The dance comes to a panting conclusion.

SIR TOBY   Dost thou think because thou art virtuous there shall be no more cakes and ale?

MALVOLIO   (*grimly*) She shall know of it. (*He points meaningly upward, and stalks away.*)

MARIA   Go shake your ears. (*She shakes her fist after the pompous steward.*) For Monsieur Malvolio, let me alone with him! If I do not gull him, do not think I have wit enough to lie straight in my bed: I know I can do it!

SIR TOBY   What wilt thou do?

MARIA   I will drop in his way some obscure epistles of love. I can write very like my lady, your niece—

SIR TOBY   Excellent, I smell a device!

SIR ANDREW   I have it in my nose too!

SIR TOBY   He shall think by the letters that thou wilt drop that they come from my niece, and that she's in love with him.

MARIA   My purpose is indeed a horse of that colour.

Maria departs.

SIR TOBY   Let's to bed, knight. Thou hadst need send for more money.

SIR ANDREW   If I cannot recover your niece, I am a foul way out.

SIR TOBY   Send for money, knight; if thou hast her not i' the end, call me cut.

In Orsino's palace, the duke has received the unhappy news of the failure of his embassy. Viola stands in attendance.

DUKE   Once more, Cesario, get thee to yon same sovereign cruelty. Tell her my love . . .

VIOLA   But if she cannot love you?

DUKE   I cannot be so answered.

VIOLA   Sooth, but you must. Say that some lady, as perhaps there is, hath for your love as great a pang of heart as you have for Olivia—

DUKE   —Make no compare between that love a woman can bear me, and that I owe Olivia!

VIOLA   Ay, but I know—

DUKE   What dost thou know?

VIOLA   Too well what love women to men may owe. My father had a daughter loved a man as it might be, perhaps, were I a woman, I should your lordship.

DUKE   And what's her history?

VIOLA   A blank, my lord. She never told her love, but let concealment, like a worm i' the bud, feed on her damask cheek; she pined in thought, and with a green and yellow melancholy she sat like Patience on a monument, smiling at grief. Was not this love indeed?

DUKE   But died thy sister of her love, my boy?

VIOLA   I am all the daughters of my father's house, and all the brothers, too—and yet I know not. Sir, shall I to this lady?

Orsino nods.

The garden of Olivia's mansion. It is a maze of intersecting paths and high box hedges. Like witty insects of the larger sort, Sir Toby, Sir Andrew and Maria scurry hither and thither and, finding a suitable path, drop a letter upon it. Then they vanish behind the hedges. Presently, solemn as an aged beetle, Malvolio comes strolling along. As he walks, he muses, and reveals to the unseen watchers, his secret self.

MALVOLIO   'Tis but fortune, all is fortune. Maria once told me she did affect me . . . To be Count Malvolio! There's an example for it: the Lady of the Strachy married the yeoman of the wardrobe. Having been three months married to her, sitting in my state— (*He sees the letter. He frowns, then glancing cautiously about him, bends and picks it up. He studies it.*) By my life, this is my lady's hand! 'To the unknown beloved.' To whom should this be? (*He breaks the seal and begins to read.*) 'Jove knows I love, but who? Lips do not move: no man must know. M.O.A.I. doth sway my life.' M.O.A.I. Every one of these letters are in my name! 'If this fall into thy hand, revolve.' (*He revolves.*) 'In my stars I am above thee, but be not afraid of greatness. Some are born great, some achieve greatness, some have greatness thrust upon 'em. Thy fates open their hands. Remember who

commended thy yellow stockings and wished to see thee ever cross-gartered: I say, remember. Go to, thou art made if thou desirest to be so; if not, let me see thee steward still.' This is open! 'Thou canst not choose to know who I am. If thou entertain'st my love, let it appear in thy smiling. Thy smiles become thee well.' Jove, I thank thee! I will smile; I will do everything that thou wilt have me!

Malvolio, overwhelmed by his good fortune, skips and capers away. The conspirators emerge from concealment, shaking with laughter and delight at the success of their plot. Maria and Sir Toby make off; Sir Andrew lingers, for he has seen that Olivia, attended by a lady, approaches. Sir Andrew steps forward and executes a courtly bow. Olivia ignores him, for she has seen Viola approaching.

VIOLA   (*bowing*) Most excellent accomplished lady, the heavens rain odours on you!

Sir Andrew backs away and secretes himself behind a hedge.

SIR ANDREW   That youth's a rare courtier—'rain odours'—well!

Olivia dismisses her companion and sits upon a rustic bench.

OLIVIA   Give me your hand, sir.

VIOLA   My duty, madam, and most humble service. (*Offers a hand. Olivia seizes it and pulls Viola to sit beside her.*) Dear lady—

OLIVIA   Give me leave, beseech you. What is your name?

VIOLA   Cesario is your servant's name, fair princess.

OLIVIA   My servant, sir? Y'are servant to the Count Orsino, youth.

VIOLA   Madam, I come to whet your gentle thoughts on his behalf—

OLIVIA   I bade you never speak of him again—

VIOLA   You'll nothing, madam, to my lord, by me? (*She tries to escape.*)

OLIVIA   Stay! Cesario, by the roses of the spring, by maidenhood, honour, truth and everything, I love thee—

VIOLA   (*at last escaping from Olivia's loving clutches*) Adieu, good madam; never more will I my master's tears to you deplore!

OLIVIA   Yet come again!

She holds out her arms to the fast vanishing Viola.

In the wine-cellar of Olivia's mansion, Sir Toby and Maria are together. They are joined by a bewildered and hurt Sir Andrew.

SIR ANDREW   I saw your niece do more favours to the count's servingman than ever she bestowed on me!

SIR TOBY   Why then, challenge me the count's youth to fight with him, hurt him in eleven places. There is no love-maker in the world can more prevail in man's commendation with women than report of valour!

MARIA   There is no way but this, Sir Andrew.

They look at one another. Sir Andrew draws his sword and flourishes it. He will take the good advice, and challenge the youth to a duel.

In the town, a perfect image of Viola is walking with a gentleman. It is Sebastian, her twin brother, who, like herself, has been saved from the sea.

SEBASTIAN   You must know of me then, Antonio, my name is Sebastian. Some hour before you took me from the breach of the sea was my sister drowned.

ANTONIO   Alas, the day!

SEBASTIAN   What's to do? Shall we go see the relics of this town?

ANTONIO   Would you'd pardon me. I do not without danger walk these streets. Once in a sea-fight 'gainst the Count his galleys, I did some service. If I be lapsed in this place I shall pay dear.

SEBASTIAN   Do not walk then too open.

ANTONIO   It doth not fit me. Hold, sir, here's my purse. In the south suburbs, at the Elephant, is best to lodge. (*He offers his purse to Sebastian.*)

SEBASTIAN   Why I your purse?

ANTONIO   Haply your eye shall light upon some toy you have desire to purchase.

SEBASTIAN   I'll be your purse-bearer and leave you for an hour . . .

They part.

In Olivia's mansion, the lady is seated with Maria.

OLIVIA   Where's Malvolio? He is sad and civil, and suits well for a servant with my fortunes. Where is Malvolio?

MARIA   (*going to the door*) He is coming, madam, but in a very strange manner.

Malvolio enters. He is solemnly black above, but riotously yellow below; and his skinny legs are imprisoned in black-cross-gartering, like starved canaries in a cage. He is smiling with great determination.

OLIVIA   (*amazed*) How now, Malvolio?

MALVOLIO   (*roguishly*) Sweet lady, ho, ho!

OLIVIA   Smil'st thou? I sent for thee upon a sad occasion.

MALVOLIO   Sad, lady? I could be sad. (*He tries to loosen his garters.*) This does make some obstruction in the blood, this cross-gartering. But what of that?

OLIVIA   What is the matter with thee? Wilt thou go to bed, Malvolio?

MALVOLIO   (*reacting with surprise and delight*) To bed? Ay, sweetheart, and I'll come to thee!

OLIVIA   What mean'st thou by that, Malvolio?

MALVOLIO   Some are born great—

OLIVIA   Ha?

MALVOLIO   Some achieve greatness—

OLIVIA   What say'st thou?

MALVOLIO   And some have greatness thrust upon them! (*He attempts to embrace Olivia who reacts with horror.*)

OLIVIA   Heavens restore thee! This is very midsummer madness!

A servant enters.

SERVANT   Madam, the young gentleman of the Count Orsino's is returned—

OLIVIA   I'll come to him. (*To Maria*) Good Maria, let this fellow be looked to. Let some of my people have a special care of him.

Exit Olivia. Sir Toby's inflamed face appears round the door, followed by the portly rest of him.

MALVOLIO   Go hang yourselves all; you are idle, shallow things, I am not of your element.

He stalks away. Sir Toby and Maria look at one another happily.

SIR TOBY   Come, we'll have him in a dark room and bound. My niece is already in the belief he's mad . . .

At the gate of the mansion where Olivia has hastened to meet Viola, and to renew her protestations of love. They have not been well received.

OLIVIA   I have said too much unto a heart of stone.

VIOLA   With the same haviour that your passion bears goes on my master's grief.

OLIVIA   Here, wear this jewel for me, 'tis my picture. Refuse it not, it hath no tongue to vex you. What shall you ask of me that I'll deny?

VIOLA   Nothing but this: your true love for my master.

OLIVIA   How with mine honour may I give him that which I have given to you?

VIOLA   (*departing*) I will acquit you.

OLIVIA   Well, come again tomorrow. Fare thee well.

Olivia retires. Viola begins to walk away, but is accosted by Sir Toby and Feste, the jester.

SIR TOBY   Gentleman, God save thee.

VIOLA   And you, sir.

SIR TOBY   That defence thou hast, betake thee to it. (*He points to Viola's sword.*)

VIOLA   (*uneasily*) You mistake, sir: I am sure no man hath any quarrel with me.

SIR TOBY   You'll find it otherwise, I assure you. Therefore, if you hold your life at any price, betake you to your guard: for your opposite has in him what youth, strength, skill and wrath, can furnish a man withal.

VIOLA   I pray you, sir, what is he?

SIR TOBY   He is a knight. Souls and bodies hath he divorced three.

VIOLA   (*trembling*) I will return again into the house. I am no fighter.

SIR TOBY   Sir, no. (*He bars Viola's way.*)

VIOLA   I beseech you, do me this courteous office, as to know of the knight what my offence to him is.

SIR TOBY   I will do so. (*He turns to Feste*) Stay by this gentleman till my return.

Sir Toby departs. Viola eyes Feste. She tries to make off. Deftly, Feste dances in front of her. There is no escape.

VIOLA   I beseech you, what manner of man is he?

FESTE   He is indeed, sir, the most skilful, bloody and fatal opposite that you could possibly have found in any part of Illyria.

While Feste is preparing Viola for the worst outside the gate, within it, Sir Toby is performing the same office for the petrified Sir Andrew.

SIR TOBY   Why, man, he is a very devil, I have not seen such a firago. They say he has been fencer to the Sophy.

SIR ANDREW   Pox on't, I'll not meddle with him!

SIR TOBY   Ay, but he will not now be pacified.

Sir Andrew tries to make off, but Sir Toby holds him fast. Outside the gate, Feste is likewise holding Viola. The gate is opened and the two combatants are thrust towards one another.

VIOLA   Pray God defend me! A little thing would make me tell them how much I lack of a man!

SIR TOBY   Come, Sir Andrew, there's no remedy.

VIOLA   I do assure you, 'tis against my will!

Viola and Sir Andrew draw swords and, with faces averted, advance towards one another. But before their blades can touch, they are interrupted. Antonio appears. Instantly, he draws his own sword and parts the duellists.

ANTONIO   Put up your sword! If this young gentleman have done offence, I'll take the fault on me!

There is general amazement; but before it can be resolved, officers come upon the scene and instantly seize Antonio.

OFFICER   Antonio, I arrest thee at the suit of Count Orsino!

ANTONIO   I must obey. (*To Viola*) This comes with seeking you. Now my necessity makes me to ask you for my purse.

Viola stares at him blankly.

OFFICER   Come, sir, away.

ANTONIO   I must entreat you for some of that money.

VIOLA   What money, sir?

ANTONIO   Will you deny me now? Is't possible that my deserts to you can lack persuasion?

VIOLA   I know of none, nor know I you by voice or any feature.

ANTONIO	O heavens themselves!
OFFICER	Come sir, I pray you go.
ANTONIO	This youth that you see here I snatched one half out of the jaws of death—
OFFICER	What's that to us? The time goes by. Away!
ANTONIO	O how vile an idol proves this god! Thou hast, Sebastian, done good feature shame.
OFFICER	The man grows mad. Away with him! Come, come, sir. (*Antonio is led away.*)
VIOLA	He named Sebastian! O if it prove, tempests are kind and salt waves fresh in love!

Before Sir Toby can stop her, she runs away.

SIR TOBY	A very dishonest paltry boy, and more coward than hare.
SIR ANDREW	I'll after him again, and beat him!

They are about to set off when, to their great surprise, their quarry approaches from the opposite direction. It is Sebastian.

SIR ANDREW	(*fiercely*) Now sir, have I met you again? There's for you!

He strikes at Sebastian with his sword. Sebastian, astonished and outraged to find himself so unreasonably set upon, returns the blow with interest.

SEBASTIAN   Why there's for thee, and there, and there!

SIR TOBY   Come on, sir, hold! (*He attempts to intervene.*)

SEBASTIAN   What wouldst thou now? Draw thy sword!

Sir Toby draws; however, at the first clash of steel, Olivia appears.

OLIVIA   Hold, Toby! on thy life, I charge thee, hold!

The combatants part.

SIR TOBY   (*contritely*) Madam!

OLIVIA   Ungracious wretch! Out of my sight! (*Sir Toby, Sir Andrew and Feste hastily depart. Olivia turns to Sebastian.*) I prithee, gentle friend, go with me to my house. (*Sebastian stands and gapes. Olivia takes him by the hand and draws him within the gate.*) Thou shalt not choose but go. Do not deny . . .

Sebastian, dazedly, suffers himself to be led by the lovely Olivia.

SEBASTIAN   If it be thus to dream, still let me sleep.

They go into the mansion.
  Even as Sebastian is in a dream of heaven, Malvolio is in a dream of hell. He has been confined, as a madman, in a dark room with a barred door. Feste, in the guise of a priest, one Sir Topaz, visits him, while Sir Toby and Maria listen eagerly to what passes, as Feste and Malvolio converse through the bars.

MALVOLIO   Do not think I am mad! They have laid me here in hideous darkness!

FESTE   Fie, thou dishonest Satan! Say'st thou the house is dark?

MALVOLIO   As hell, Sir Topaz!

FESTE   Madman, thou errest. There is no darkness but ignorance. Fare thee well.

MALVOLIO   Sir Topaz, Sir Topaz!

SIR TOBY   To him, in thine own voice! (*Sir Toby and Maria depart.*)

FESTE   (*in his own voice*) Alas, sir, how fell you beside your five wits?

MALVOLIO   I am as well in my wits, fool, as thou art.

FESTE   But as well? Then you are mad indeed, if you be no better in your wits than a fool!

MALVOLIO   Good fool, help me to some light and some paper. I tell thee I am as well in my wits as any man in Illyria! Some ink, paper and light, and convey what I will set down to my lady!

FESTE   (*sings*)

I am gone, sir, and anon, sir,
I'll be with you again . . .

In Olivia's garden, Sebastian muses on his good fortune.

SEBASTIAN   This may be some error, but no madness, yet doth this accident and flood of fortune so far exceed all instance, all discourse, that I am ready to distrust mine eyes, and wrangle with my reason that persuades me to any other trust but that I am mad, or else the lady's mad . . . But here the lady comes!

Olivia approaches, dragging in her wake, a priest, a real one.

OLIVIA   Blame not this haste of mine. If you mean well, now go with me and with this holy man into the chantry by; there before him, plight me the full assurance of your faith. What do you say?

Sebastian stares about him, as if weighing up all the advantages of the match.

SEBASTIAN   I'll follow this good man, and go with you, and having sworn truth, ever will be true.

OLIVIA   Then lead the way, good father.

Vigorously, she propels the priest towards the chapel wherein all her dreams will soon come true.

Outside the gate of the mansion, the duke and Viola, with lords in attendance, approach. Feste, leaning against the gatepost, bows and holds out his hand. The duke drops a coin into it.

DUKE
If you will let your lady know I am here to speak with her, and bring her along with you, it may awaken my bounty further.

Feste departs into the house. A group of officers approach. In their midst is their prisoner, Antonio.

VIOLA
Here comes the man, sir, that did rescue me.

OFFICER
Orsino, this is that Antonio that took the Phoenix—

VIOLA
He did me kindness, sir—

DUKE
Notable pirate, what foolish boldness brought thee—

ANTONIO
A witchcraft drew me hither. That most ungrateful boy there by your side! For his sake did I expose myself into the danger of this adverse town; drew to defend him when he was beset; where, being apprehended, his false cunning denied me mine own purse, which I had recommended to his use not half an hour before!

VIOLA
How can this be?

Olivia, attended, appears at the gate. She sees Viola.

OLIVIA   Cesario, you do not keep promise with me.

VIOLA   Madam—

DUKE   Gracious Olivia—

OLIVIA   (*ignoring the duke*) What do you say, Cesario?

VIOLA   My lord would speak—

OLIVIA   If it be aught to the old tune, my lord, it is as fat and fulsome to mine ear as howling after music.

DUKE   Still so cruel?

OLIVIA   Still so constant, my lord.

     Orsino sighs, and turns to Viola

DUKE   Come, boy, with me. (*The duke turns to leave. Viola does likewise.*)

OLIVIA   Where goes Cesario?

VIOLA   After him I love.

OLIVIA   Hast thou forgot thyself? Is it so long?

DUKE   Come away.

OLIVIA   Cesario, husband, stay!

DUKE   Husband?

OLIVIA   Ay, husband. Can he deny?

DUKE   (*to Viola*) Her husband, sirrah?

VIOLA   Not I, my lord!

As all look to one another in disgust, anger, and uncomprehending terror, the priest appears.

OLIVIA   O welcome, father! I charge thee, by thy reverence, here to unfold what thou dost know hath newly passed between this youth and me.

PRIEST   A contract of eternal bond of love—

DUKE   O thou dissembling cub! Farewell, and take her—

VIOLA   (*in tears*) My lord, I do protest—

Sir Andrew comes staggering, bleeding from his head.

SIR ANDREW   (*gasping*) For the love of God, a surgeon! Send one presently to Sir Toby!

OLIVIA   Who has done this, Sir Andrew?

SIR ANDREW   The Count's gentleman, one Cesario. 'Od's lifelings, here he is! You broke my head for nothing!

VIOLA   Why do you speak to me? I never hurt you.

Now comes Sir Toby, also bleeding, and assisted by Feste.

DUKE   How now, gentleman, how is't with you?

SIR TOBY   That's all one. H'as hurt me, (*pointing to Viola*) and there's th'end on't.

OLIVIA   Get him to bed, and let his hurt be looked to.

Sir Andrew, Sir Toby and Feste depart. No sooner have they gone than Sebastian appears.

SEBASTIAN   I am sorry, madam, I have hurt your kinsman: But had it been the brother of my blood, I must have done no less with wit and safety. You throw a strange regard upon me, and by that I do perceive it hath offended you. Pardon me, sweet one, even for the vows we made each other but so late ago.

All are suddenly dumb with amazement, as they look from Sebastian to Viola.

DUKE   One face, one voice, one habit, and two persons! A natural perspective, that is, and is not!

SEBASTIAN   (*seeing Antonio*) Antonio, O my dear Antonio! How have the hours racked and tortured me, since I have lost thee!

ANTONIO   Sebastian are you?

OLIVIA   Most wonderful!

Sebastian and Viola now see one another.

SEBASTIAN   Do I stand there? I never had a brother. What kin are you to me?

VIOLA   Sebastian was my father; such a Sebastian was my brother too: so went he suited to his watery tomb. If spirits can assume both form and suit, you come to fright us.

SEBASTIAN   Thrice welcome, drowned Viola! (*To Olivia*) So comes it, lady, you have been mistook. You would have been contracted to a maid; nor are you therein, by my life, deceived: you are betrothed both to a maid and man.

Olivia stares uncertainly at her husband.

DUKE   Be not amazed, right noble is his blood. (*Olivia and Sebastian join hands.*) If this be so, as yet the glass seems true, I shall have share in this most happy wreck. (*To Viola*) Boy, thou hast said to me a thousand times thou never shouldst love woman like me.

VIOLA   And all those sayings will I over-swear!

DUKE   Give me thy hand. You shall from this time be your master's mistress!

OLIVIA   (*gazing from Sebastian to Viola*) A sister! You are she!

In the midst of all the embracings and smiles comes Malvolio, unkempt, with straw in his hair and rage in his eyes. Feste follows.

MALVOLIO Madam, you have done me wrong, notorious wrong!

OLIVIA   Have I, Malvolio? No.

MALVOLIO   Lady, you have. Pray you, peruse that letter. (*Gives her the fatal letter.*) You must not now deny it is your hand. Tell me, in the modesty of honour, why you have given me such clear lights of favour, bade me come smiling and cross-gartered to you? Why have you suffered me to be imprisoned, kept in a dark house? Tell me, why?

OLIVIA   Alas, Malvolio, this is not my writing—

FESTE   Good madam, hear me speak. Most freely I confess, myself and Toby set this device against Malvolio here. Maria writ the letter, at Sir Toby's great importance, in recompense whereof he hath married her—

OLIVIA   Alas, poor fool, how have they baffled thee.

MALVOLIO   I'll be revenged on the whole pack of you!

He stalks away in high indignation.

OLIVIA   He hath been most notoriously abused.

DUKE   Pursue him, and entreat him to a peace. Cesario, come; for so you shall be while you are a man; but when in other habits you are seen, Orsino's mistress and his fancy's queen.

The lovers, in pairs, go within the mansion gates. Only Feste is left behind. He seats himself outside the gate and sings:

FESTE

When that I was and a little tiny boy,
With hey, ho, the wind and the rain,
A foolish thing was but a toy,
For the rain it raineth every day.
But when I came to man's estate,
With hey, ho, the wind and the rain,
'Gainst knaves and thieves men shut their gate,
For the rain it raineth every day.
A great while ago the world begun,
With hey, ho, the wind and the rain,
But that's all one, our play is done,
And we'll strive to please you every day.

The curtain falls . . .

A MIDSUMMER NIGHT'S DREAM

The curtain rises on Athens, a white and golden city, bright and joyous as a wedding cake. Everywhere there is preparation for the marriage of Duke Theseus to Hippolyta, the queen he has won in battle. But in the midst of all this happiness, there is a speck of misery, like a sour plum . . .

   Into the council chamber of the palace, an angry father, Egeus, drags his disobedient daughter, Hermia, to seek justice before the duke and his royal bride.

   She will not marry the man of his choice but obstinately prefers another.

   After them come the two young men in question: Lysander, the daughter's desire and Demetrius, her father's. Wilfully, she breaks free of Egeus's grasp.

EGEUS   Happy be Theseus, our renowned Duke! Full of vexation come I, with complaint against my child, my daughter Hermia. Stand forth, Demetrius! (*Demetrius, full of virtue, stands forth.*) My noble lord, this man hath my consent to marry her. Stand forth, Lysander! (*Lysander, full of defiance, stands forth.*) And, my gracious Duke, this man hath bewitched the bosom of my child. (*Lysander and Hermia exchange ardent looks.*) Be it so she will not here, before your grace, consent to marry with Demetrius, I beg the ancient privilege of Athens; as she is mine, I may dispose of her, either to this gentleman or to her death.

THESEUS   Be advised, fair maid. Demetrius is a worthy gentleman.

HERMIA   So is Lysander. I do entreat your grace to pardon me. But I beseech your grace that I may know the worst that may befall me in this case, if I refuse to wed Demetrius.

THESEUS   Either to die the death, or to abjure for ever the society of men. Take time to pause—

Hermia and Lysander gaze at each other.

DEMETRIUS   Relent, sweet Hermia; and Lysander, yield—

LYSANDER   You have her father's love, Demetrius, let me have Hermia's —do you marry him. (*To the duke*) I am, my lord, as well-derived as he, and, which is more, I am beloved of beauteous Hermia. Demetrius, I'll avouch it to his head, made love to Nedar's daughter, Helena, and won her soul.

THESEUS   I must confess that I have heard so much. But Demetrius, come, and come, Egeus. You shall go with me. For you, fair Hermia, look you arm yourself to fit your fancies to your father's will.

They all depart, leaving Hermia and Lysander alone.

LYSANDER   Ay me! The course of true love never did run smooth.

HERMIA   If then true lovers have been ever crossed, it stands as an edict in destiny.

LYSANDER   So quick bright things come to confusion. If thou lov'st me, then steal forth thy father's house tomorrow night, and in the wood, a league without the town, there will I stay for thee.

HERMIA   I swear to thee by Cupid's strongest bow, tomorrow truly will I meet with thee.

LYSANDER   Keep promise, love. Look, here comes Helena!

Helena enters, much distracted, for she loves Demetrius even as Hermia loves Lysander but alas with no return.

HERMIA   God speed, fair Helena! Whither away?

HELENA   Call you me fair? That 'fair' again unsay. O teach me how you look, and with what art you sway the motion of Demetrius' heart.

HERMIA   Take comfort: he no more shall see my face.

LYSANDER   Tomorrow night through Athens' gates have we devised to steal.

HERMIA   And in the wood where often you and I were wont to lie, there my Lysander and myself shall meet. Farewell, sweet playfellow; pray thou for us!

They all part. Helena lingers and gazes bitterly after Hermia.

HELENA   Ere Demetrius looked on Hermia's eyne, he hailed down oaths that he was only mine. I will go tell him of fair Hermia's flight! (*Vindictively*) Then to the wood . . .

So while the preparations for the wedding of Duke Theseus occupy his subjects, the four lovers flee the city. Meanwhile, in a humble, smoky, candlelit room, six worthy workmen of Athens are gathered together. They are to prepare a play for the festivities of the wedding. If they succeed, they will all be given pensions for life; so it is a serious business. The play has been chosen: it is Pyramus and Thisbe, a tale of tragic lovers.

The company is to be directed by Peter Quince, the carpenter. Foremost among his actors is Nick Bottom, the weaver. The lesser lights are Flute, the bellows-mender, Snout, the tinker, Snug, the joiner, and Starveling, the tailor.

QUINCE   Is all our company here? (*They nod.*) Here is the scroll of every man's name which is thought fit through all Athens to play in our interlude before the Duke and Duchess on his wedding day at night. Answer me as I call you. Nick Bottom, the weaver?

BOTTOM   Ready. Name what part I am for, and proceed.

QUINCE   You, Nick Bottom, are set down for Pyramus.

BOTTOM   What is Pyramus? A lover or a tyrant?

QUINCE   A lover that kills himself, most gallant, for love. Francis Flute, the bellows-mender?

FLUTE   Here, Peter Quince.

QUINCE   Flute, you must take Thisbe on you.

FLUTE   Nay, faith, let me not play a woman: I have a beard coming.

QUINCE   That's all one: you shall play it in a mask—

BOTTOM   Let me play Thisbe too—

QUINCE   No, no; you must play Pyramus; and Flute, you Thisbe. Robin Starveling, the tailor? You must play Thisbe's mother. Tom Snout, the tinker? You, Pyramus' father; myself, Thisbe's father; Snug, the joiner, you the lion's part.

SNUG   Have you the lion's part written? Pray you, if it be, give it to me, for I am slow of study.

QUINCE   You may do it extempore; for it is nothing but roaring.

BOTTOM   Let me play the lion too. I will roar that I will make the Duke say, 'Let him roar again!'

QUINCE   You can play no part but Pyramus; for Pyramus is a sweet-faced man.

BOTTOM   Well, I will undertake it.

QUINCE   Here are your parts, (*he distributes scrolls*) and I am to entreat you to con them by tomorrow night, and meet me in the palace wood by moonlight; there will we rehearse . . .

The wood. The moon shines down and tips all the leaves with silver. It is a place of mystery. Unseen creatures rustle among the bushes, like disturbed dreams. Suddenly, in a clearing, a weird configuration of tree and leaf becomes a strange, threatening figure in a dark cloak. It is Oberon, king of the night-time world. At his feet crouches Puck, his wicked, grinning henchman, and all about are his sharp-eyed goblin servants.

OBERON   Ill met by moonlight, proud Titania.

Across the glade appears the delicate, glittering fairy queen, accompanied by her glimmering train of sprites. Among them is a pretty little Indian boy, guarded like a jewel. The fairy king and queen stare at one another with hostility.

TITANIA   What, jealous Oberon? Fairies, skip hence! I have forsworn his bed and company. (*She raises her hand. Her followers quiver and tremble to depart.*)

OBERON   Tarry, rash wanton! Why should Titania cross her Oberon? I do but beg a little changeling boy to be my henchman. (*He points to the Indian child.*)

TITANIA   Set your heart at rest. The fairy land buys not the child of me. His mother was a votaress of my order . . .

OBERON   Give me that boy!

TITANIA   Not for thy fairy kingdom! Fairies, away!

With a screaming and rushing sound Titania and her train vanish from the glade.

OBERON   Well, go thy way; thou shalt not from this grove till I torment thee for this injury. My gentle Puck, come hither . . . (*Puck approaches, Oberon whispers in his crooked ear.*) Fetch me that flower, the herb I showed thee once; the juice of it on sleeping eyelids laid will make or man or woman madly dote upon the next live creature that it sees. Fetch me this herb!

PUCK   I'll put a girdle round about the earth in forty minutes!

Like a whirling leaf, Puck flies off. Oberon smiles.

OBERON   Having once this juice I'll watch Titania when she is asleep, and drop the liquor of it in her eyes; the next thing then she, waking, looks upon—be it on lion, bear or wolf, or bull, on meddling monkey, or on busy ape—she shall pursue it with the soul of love—

He is disturbed by a sudden crashing of branches. Instantly, he becomes invisible. The crashing grows louder and first Demetrius, then Helena, burst into the glade.

DEMETRIUS   I love thee not, therefore pursue me not! Where is Lysander and fair Hermia? Hence, get thee gone, and follow me no more.

HELENA   (*clutching tearfully at him*) I am your spaniel; and Demetrius, the more you beat me, I will fawn on you. Use me but as your spaniel, spurn me, strike me, neglect me, lose me; only give me leave, unworthy as I am, to follow you!

DEMETRIUS   (*flinging her off*) I am sick when I do look on thee!

HELENA   (*clutching him again*) And I am sick when I look not on you!

DEMETRIUS   Let me go, or, if thou follow me, do not believe but I shall do thee mischief in the wood!

He escapes and plunges away into the wood. Helena follows, weeping. Oberon becomes visible again.

OBERON   Fare thee well, nymph. Ere he do leave this grove, thou shalt fly him, and he shall seek thy love.

Puck returns, as swiftly as he departed. He kneels at his master's feet, and holds up a purple flower. Oberon takes it and gazes at it, musingly.

OBERON   I know a bank where the wild thyme blows, where oxlips and the nodding violet grows, quite over-canopied with luscious woodbine, with sweet musk-roses and with eglantine. There sleeps Titania some time of the night . . . (*He peers into the depths of the flower.*) With the juice of this I'll streak her eyes, and make her full of hateful fantasies. (*Puck laughs delightedly. Oberon frowns. He takes a petal from the flower and gives it to Puck.*) Take thou some of it, and seek through this grove: a sweet Athenian lady is in love with a disdainful youth; anoint his eyes; but do it when the next thing he espies may be the lady. Thou shalt know the man by the Athenian garments he hath on.

PUCK   Fear not, my lord, your servant shall do so.

Another part of the moonlit wood: the 'bank where the wild thyme blows'. Titania reclines upon a mossy couch. Her attendants watch over her, and her Indian boy plays happily . . .

TITANIA   Come now, a roundel and a fairy song . . .

ATTENDANTS   You spotted snakes with double tongue,
Thorny hedgehogs be not seen;
Newts and blindworms do no wrong,
Come not near our fairy queen . . .

As they sing, Titania closes her eyes and sleeps. The attendants creep away, taking with them the Indian boy. Titania is alone. Suddenly Oberon appears. He smiles, and, bending over his sleeping queen, squeezes the magic liquor from the flower upon her eyelids.

OBERON   What thou seest when thou dost wake, do it for thy true love take. Wake when some vile thing is near.

Slowly, Oberon vanishes. Titania sleeps on, 'quite over-canopied with luscious woodbine'. Slowly, she fades into invisibility. Into the glade, arm in loving arm, come Hermia and Lysander. They are plainly weary from walking.

LYSANDER   We'll rest us, Hermia, if you think it good.

HERMIA   Be it so, Lysander; find you out a bed, for I upon this couch will rest my head.

She seats herself. Lysander promptly sits beside her, very close.

LYSANDER   One turf shall serve as pillow for us both.

HERMIA   Nay, good Lysander; for my sake, my dear, lie further off yet.

He retires, but not by much. Hermia gestures urgently.

HERMIA   Lie further off, in human modesty; such separation as may well be said becomes a virtuous bachelor and a maid. (*Lysander at last betakes himself to a satisfactory distance.*) So far be distant; and good night, sweet friend.

They both settle down and, in moments, are asleep. No sooner are their eyes closed than Puck appears.

PUCK
There is he my master said despised the Athenian maid; and here the maiden, sleeping sound, on the dank and dirty ground. Pretty soul, she durst not lie near this lack-love, this kill-courtesy! (*He bends over Lysander and anoints his eyes with juice from the magic flower.*) Churl, upon thine eyes I throw all the power this charm doth owe.

Sounds of a violent approach cause Puck to vanish abruptly. Into the glade rushes Demetrius, followed by the weeping, brush-torn Helena.

DEMETRIUS
I charge thee, hence, and do not haunt me thus!

He plunges on, Helena pauses, and stares fearfully about her.

HELENA
O wilt thou darkling leave me? (*Suddenly she spies Lysander.*) But who is here? Lysander on the ground? Dead, or asleep? I see no blood, no wound. Lysander, if you live, good sir, awake!

She bends low over him, and gently shakes him. He opens his magically anointed eyes. Instantly he falls in love with Helena. He looks towards the sleeping Hermia. He frowns and shakes his head. He looks again at Helena, now radiant in his eyes.

LYSANDER   Not Hermia, but Helena I love: who will not change a raven for a dove!

He rises and tries to embrace her. Helena leaps back with a squeal of alarm.

HELENA   Good troth, you do me wrong, good sooth, you do! Fare you well!

She flies from the glade in great distress. Lysander stares at the sleeping Hermia. His expression is far from loving.

LYSANDER   Hermia, sleep thou there, and never mayest thou come Lysander near! (*He gazes after the departed Helena.*) All my powers, address your love and might, to honour Helen and to be her knight!

He pursues Helena. Hermia is left alone. She stirs and frowns, in the grip of a bad dream. She cries out in her sleep—

HERMIA   Help me, Lysander, help me! Pluck this crawling serpent from my breast! (*She wakes.*) Ay me, for pity! What a dream was there! (*She looks about her.*) Lysander! Lysander, lord! Alack, where are you! (*She rises and rushes from the glade.*)

For a moment, the place is quiet; then comes the tramp of sturdy feet and, one by one, the Athenian workmen, bearing their scrolls, enter the glade.

QUINCE   Here's a marvellous convenient place for our rehearsal.

BOTTOM   (*consulting his scroll*) Peter Quince, there are things in this comedy of Pyramus and Thisbe that will never please. First, Pyramus must draw a sword to kill himself, which the ladies cannot abide.

STARVELING   I believe we must leave the killing out, when all is done.

BOTTOM   Not a whit; I have a device to make all well. Write 'em a prologue, and let the prologue seem to say we will do no harm with our swords, and that Pyramus is not killed indeed; and for the more better assurance, tell him that I, Pyramus, am not Pyramus, but Bottom the weaver: this will put them out of fear.

QUINCE   Well, it shall be so. But there is two hard things: that is, to bring moonlight into a chamber; for, you know, Pyramus and Thisbe meet by moonlight.

BOTTOM   Why, then, you must leave a casement of the great chamber window, where we play, open—

QUINCE   Ay, or else one must come in with a bush of thorn and a lantern, and say he comes to disfigure, or to present the person of Moonshine. (*All nod wisely*.) Then there is another thing: we must have a wall in the great chamber; for Pyramus and Thisbe (says the story) did talk through the chink of a wall.

SNOUT   You can never bring in a wall. What say you, Bottom?

BOTTOM   Some man or other must present Wall; and let him have some plaster, or some loam, or some rough-cast about him to signify Wall.

QUINCE   If that may be, then all is well. Come, sit down every mother's son, and rehearse your parts. Pyramus, you begin . . .

They disperse themselves about the glade. Puck appears, in grinning invisibility.

PUCK   What hempen homespuns have we swaggering here, so near the cradle of the Fairy Queen? (*He stays to observe.*)

QUINCE   Speak, Pyramus! Thisbe, stand forth!

Bottom and Flute confront one another.

BOTTOM   Thisbe, the flowers of odious savours sweet—

QUINCE   Odorous—odorous!

BOTTOM   . . . odorous savours sweet. So hath thy breath, my dearest Thisbe dear. (*Quince thumps on the ground, as a cue.*) But hark, a voice. Stay thou but here awhile, and by and by I will to thee appear. (*Exit Bottom into a bush, above which hovers Puck.*)

FLUTE   Must I speak now?

QUINCE   Ay, marry, must you!

FLUTE   (*girlishly*) Most radiant Pyramus, most lily-white of hue! I'll meet thee, Pyramus, at Ninny's tomb.

QUINCE   At Ninus's tomb, man! Why, you must not speak yet; that you must answer to Pyramus. You speak all your part at once, cues and all! (*He turns to the bush*) Pyramus, enter! Your cue is past—

As he speaks, Puck, still hovering above the bush, makes a magic pass with his hands. A pair of large, hairy ears appears, poking through the leaves.

QUINCE   Pyramus, enter!

A loud thumping, and Bottom emerges from the bush. But a strangely altered Bottom. In place of his human head is now the head of an ass!

BOTTOM   If I were fair, Thisbe—

Bottom's companions stare at him in stark terror.

QUINCE   O monstrous! O strange! We are haunted! Pray, masters! Fly, masters! Help!

They fly madly from the glade, leaving the weirdly altered Bottom alone.

BOTTOM   Why do they run away?

Briefly, Quince returns, as if to make sure of what he has seen.

QUINCE   Bless thee, Bottom, bless thee! Thou art translated! (*He departs.*)

BOTTOM   I see their knavery: this is to make an ass of me, to fright me if they could . . . (*He begins to walk up and down, to keep his spirits up.*) I will sing, that they shall hear I am not afraid:

> The ousel cock, so black of hue,
> With orange-tawny bill,
> The throstle with his note so true,
> The wren with little quill . . .

As he sings, Titania, sleeping on her mossy couch, becomes visible. Skilfully, Puck leads the singing Bottom towards the Fairy Queen. Titania awakes, and feasts her magically anointed eyes upon the donkey-headed Bottom.

TITANIA   What angel wakes me from my flowery bed? I pray thee, gentle mortal, sing again: mine ear is much enamoured of thy note. So is mine eye enthralled to thy shape, and thy fair virtue's force perforce doth move me on first view to say, to swear, I love thee.

Bottom gazes at the Fairy Queen without surprise; indeed, it would take much to surprise Bottom.

BOTTOM   Methinks, mistress, you should have little reason for that. And yet, to say the truth, reason and love keep little company nowadays. The more the pity that some honest neighbours will not make them friends.

Titania's attendants look on in amazement at this mad infatuation of their mistress. Titania rises from the ground and takes Bottom by the arm.

TITANIA   Thou art as wise as thou art beautiful.

BOTTOM   Not so neither; but if I had wit enough to get out of this wood, I had enough to serve mine own turn.

TITANIA   Out of this wood do not desire to go. Thou shalt remain here, whether thou wilt or no. I am a spirit of no common rate; and I do love thee: therefore go with me. I'll give thee fairies to attend on thee.

She signs to her followers, who obediently attend on Bottom. They all leave the glade, leaving behind the forgotten little Indian boy.

Another part of the wood. Oberon and Puck are together. Puck is helpless with laughter.

PUCK   My mistress with a monster is in love!

OBERON   This falls out better than I could devise. But hast thou yet latched the Athenian's eyes with the love-juice?

PUCK   I took him sleeping—

They are interrupted by the entry of Hermia, amorously pursued by Demetrius. Instantly, Puck and Oberon become invisible.

OBERON   Stand close; this is the same Athenian.

PUCK   This is the woman, but not this the man.

HERMIA   Out, dog; out, cur! Hast thou slain him then?

DEMETRIUS   I am not guilty of Lysander's blood!

HERMIA   See me no more, whether he be dead or no!

She flies from him.

DEMETRIUS   There is no following her in this fierce vein . . .

He sighs and sinks to the ground. He sleeps. Oberon and Puck reappear. Oberon remonstrates.

OBERON   What hast thou done? Thou hast mistaken quite, and laid the love-juice on some true love's sight. About the wood go swifter than the wind, and Helena of Athens look thou find!

PUCK   I go, I go, look how I go! Swifter than arrow from the Tartar's bow!

With a rush of leaves, as of a sudden wind, Puck flies off. Oberon bends over the sleeping Demetrius and anoints his eyes with liquor from the magic flower.

OBERON   Flower of this purple dye, hit with Cupid's archery, sink in th' apple of his eye. When his love he doth espy—

Puck returns, mightily out of breath.

PUCK   Captain of our fairy band, Helena is here at hand.

Oberon and Puck become invisible as the weeping Helena, still followed by the ardent Lysander, comes into the glade. Helena almost falls over the sleeping Demetrius, who wakes and, seeing her, instantly falls in love with her.

DEMETRIUS   O Helen, goddess, nymph, perfect, divine!

He tries to embrace her. Alarmed, she backs away . . . into the waiting arms of Lysander! She cries out and frees herself. She stares, tearfully, from one young man to the other.

HELENA	O spite! O hell! I see you are all bent to set against me for your merriment! You are both rivals, and love Hermia—
DEMETRIUS	Lysander, keep thy Hermia! If ere I loved her, all that love is gone, and now to Helen is it home returned!
LYSANDER	Helen, it is not so—
DEMETRIUS	Look where thy love comes; yonder is thy dear!

Enter Hermia. She rushes to Lysander.

HERMIA	Lysander, why unkindly didst thou leave me so?
LYSANDER	(*pushing her away*) Why seek'st thou me? Could not this make thee know the hate I bear thee made me leave thee so?
HERMIA	Hate me? Wherefore? Am I not Hermia? Are not you Lysander?
LYSANDER	Ay, by my life; and never did desire to see thee more. Be certain, nothing truer—that I do hate thee and love Helena.

Hermia stares at Helena, who, flanked by her two new lovers, smiles feebly.

HERMIA	You juggler! You canker-blossom! You thief of love!
HELENA	Have you no modesty, no maiden shame? You puppet, you!
HERMIA	Puppet? Thou painted maypole!

*She launches herself furiously upon Helena, who skips behind
the young men.*

HELENA   Let her not hurt me! O, when she is angry, she is keen and
shrewd. She was a vixen when she went to school!

HERMIA   Let me come at her!

LYSANDER   Get you gone, you dwarf!

*He tries to comfort the terrified Helena. Demetrius pushes him
aside. Lysander draws his sword. Demetrius does likewise.
They circle each other, and, still threatening, back out of the
glade. Hermia and Helena glare at each other.*

HERMIA   You, mistress—

HELENA   (*backing away*) Your hands than mine are quicker for a fray;
my legs are longer, though, to run away!

*She bolts from the glade. Hermia pursues. Oberon and Puck
reappear.*

PUCK   Lord, what fools these mortals be!

OBERON   This is thy negligence; still thou mistak'st, or else commits thy
knaveries wilfully.

PUCK   Believe me, king of shadows, I mistook.

OBERON   Thou seest these lovers seek a place to fight. Hie therefore, Robin, overcast the night . . . and lead these testy rivals so astray, as one come not within another's way . . . till o'er their brows death-counterfeiting sleep with leaden legs and batty wings doth creep. (*He gives Puck another flower.*) Then crush this herb into Lysander's eye . . .

As Puck, with magic signs, overcasts the night, a thick black fog begins to invade the wood, turning the trees to ghosts and the bushes to crouching bears. Lysander and Demetrius, no longer able to see one another, stumble on, while Puck taunts each of the rivals with the other's voice. At last, they collapse on the ground, quite overcome with weariness. Similarly, Helena and Hermia, pursued and pursuer, sink down and fall asleep. Puck, his work all but done, bends low over Lysander, and crushes the herb upon his eyelids.

PUCK   When thou wak'st, thou tak'st true delight in the sight of thy former lady's eye; and the country proverb known, that every man should take his own, in your waking shall be shown. Jack shall have Jill, naught shall go ill . . .

Puck gazes at the four sleeping lovers then fades away.

In Titania's glade, the Fairy Queen is entertaining her fantastical love. Donkey-headed Bottom, wreathed in flowers, reclines in Titania's arms, while her attendants gently fan him and tickle his hairy ears. The Indian boy plays on his own.

TITANIA   Sweet love, what desir'st thou to eat?

BOTTOM   Truly, a peck of provender; I could munch dry oats. (*He yawns.*) But I pray you, let none of your people stir me; I have an exposition of sleep come upon me.

TITANIA   Sleep thou, and I will wind thee in my arms. O how I love thee! How I dote on thee!

The attendants steal away as the strange lovers sleep. Oberon appears, with Puck. He looks with pity on the unnatural scene. He sees the Indian boy. He nods to Puck, who bears the child away.

OBERON   Now I have the boy, I will undo this hateful imperfection of her eyes . . . (*He squeezes the herb into Titania's sleeping eyes.*) Be as thou wast wont to be; see as thou wast wont to see . . .

Titania opens her eyes.

TITANIA	My Oberon! what visions have I seen! Methought I was enamoured of an ass!
OBERON	There lies your love!

Titania, seeing the sleeping Bottom, shudders. Puck returns. Oberon nods, and Puck restores Bottom to his proper human shape. Titania seems unimpressed by the improvement.

PUCK	Now when thou wak'st, with thine own fool's eyes peep.
OBERON	Come, my queen, take hands with me . . .

Oberon and Titania join hands, and, with Puck and all their returning attendants, dance away. Bottom is left alone, fast asleep and smiling.

Now that the creatures of the night have gone, thin arrows of daylight begin to pierce the wood. There are sounds of hunting horns, and hounds baying. Duke Theseus, with Hippolyta and courtiers, all attired for the hunt, appear.

THESEUS   The music of my hounds!

HIPPOLYTA   I was with Hercules and Cadmus once, with hounds of Sparta. I never heard so musical a discord, such sweet thunder.

THESEUS   My hounds are bred out of the Spartan kind; so flew'd, so sanded; and their heads are hung with ears that sweep away the morning dew; slow in pursuit; but matched in mouth like bells, each under each. A cry more tuneable was never hallooed to nor cheered with horn— (*He sees the four lovers, still sleeping.*) But soft, what nymphs are these?

Hermia's father, Egeus, is of the company. Angrily he examines the sleepers.

EGEUS   My lord, this is my daughter here asleep. And this Lysander; this Demetrius is, and this Helena.

THESEUS   Go bid the huntsmen wake them with their horns. (*Obediently, the horns bray out. The lovers awake in some confusion. They see the duke, and at once rise and kneel before him.*) I pray you, all stand up.

They stand, Lysander with Hermia, and Demetrius with Helena. Egeus tries to drag his daughter away from her love. She will not come. Egeus points furiously at Lysander, and addresses the duke.

EGEUS   I beg the law, the law upon his head!

Theseus gazes at the four lovers, and smiles.

THESEUS   Fair lovers, you are fortunately met. Egeus, I will overbear your will; for in the temple, by and by, with us, these couples shall eternally be knit. (*Egeus bows his head and resigns himself to the duke's decree.*) Away with us, to Athens: three and three, we'll hold a feast in great solemnity.

Theseus and his followers leave the glade. The four lovers gaze wonderingly at one another.

DEMETRIUS   These things seem small and indistinguishable, like far-off mountains turned into clouds.

HERMIA   Methinks I see these things with parted eye, when everything seems double.

HELENA   So methinks . . .

DEMETRIUS   Are you sure that we are awake? It seems to me that yet we sleep, we dream. Do not you think the Duke was here?

LYSANDER   And he did bid us follow to the temple.

DEMETRIUS   Why, then, we are awake. Let's follow him, and by the way let us recount our dreams.

In the glade once inhabited by the Fairy Queen lies Bottom, still asleep. Then he, too, awakes, with a start.

BOTTOM   When my cue comes, call me and I will answer. My next is, 'most fair Pyramus—' (*He stops and stares about him.*) Peter Quince? Flute, the bellows-mender? Snout, the tinker? Starveling? God's my life! Stolen hence and left me asleep! (*He touches his head, and fumbles uneasily for his ears. Finding them to be human ears, he sighs with relief.*) I have had a most rare vision. (*He gazes towards the mossy couch upon which he lay with Titania. He smiles.*) I have had a dream . . . I will get Peter Quince to write a ballad of this dream; it shall be called 'Bottom's Dream', because it hath no bottom . . .

Back in Athens, in their smoky, candlelit room, Peter Quince and his companions are sorely distressed.

QUINCE   Have you sent to Bottom's house?

STARVELING He cannot be heard of.

FLUTE   If he come not, the play is marred . . .

QUINCE   You have not a man in all Athens able to discharge Pyramus but he.

SNUG   If our sport had gone forward, we had all been made men.

FLUTE   O sweet bully Bottom! Thus hath he lost sixpence a day during his life. Sixpence a day in Pyramus, or nothing.

Even as they all mourn the loss of their chief hope, their star of stars, the door bursts open and Bottom himself stands in the doorway. Panting from running, he surveys his fellows, beaming proudly.

BOTTOM   Where are these lads? Where are these hearts?

QUINCE   Bottom! O most courageous day! O most happy hour!

BOTTOM   Get your apparel together! Every man look o'er his part; for the short and the long is, our play is preferred! Let Thisbe have clean linen, and let not him that plays the lion pare his nails. And, most dear actors, eat no onions nor garlic, for we are to utter sweet breath. No more words. Away!

In the royal palace, Theseus and Hippolyta, seated in state and attended by courtiers, await the night's entertainment.

HIPPOLYTA   'Tis strange, my Theseus, that these lovers speak of.

THESEUS   More strange than true. The lunatic, the lover, and the poet are of imagination all compact. One sees more devils than vast hell can hold; that is the madman. The lover, all as frantic, sees Helen's beauty in a brow of Egypt. The poet's eye, in a fine frenzy rolling, doth glance from heaven to earth, from earth to heaven, and as imagination bodies forth the forms of things unknown, the poet's pen turns them to shapes, and gives to airy nothing a local habitation and a name. Such tricks hath strong imagination—

HIPPOLYTA   But all the story of the night told over, and all their minds transfigured so together, more witnesseth than fancy's images, and grows to something of great constancy; but howsoever, strange and admirable.

The four lovers enter, and Theseus bids them seat themselves and prepare to be entertained. Philostrate, the Master of Revels, steps forward.

PHILOSTRATE A play there is, my lord, some ten words long, which is as brief as I have known a play; but by ten words, my lord, it is too long.

THESEUS What are they that do play it?

PHILOSTRATE Hard-handed men that work in Athens here, which never laboured in their minds till now.

THESEUS I will hear that play; for never anything can be amiss, when simpleness and duty tender it.

Philostrate bows and withdraws. Presently he ushers in Peter Quince and his company. They are all in costume, even to the man in the moon and the wall.

QUINCE Gentles, perchance you wonder at this show; but wonder on till truth make all things plain. This man is Pyramus, if you would know; this beauteous lady Thisbe is certain; this man with lime and rough-cast, doth present Wall, that vile wall which did these lovers sunder; this man with lantern, dog and bush of thorn, presenteth Moonshine. This grisly beast, which Lion hight by name . . .

Great applause for the lion. The action of the play commences.

THESEUS Pyramus draws near the wall; silence!

Bottom, attired as Pyramus, creeps towards Snout, the Wall.

BOTTOM Thou wall, O wall, O sweet and lovely wall, show me thy chink to blink through with mine eye.

Snout's two fingers are raised for Bottom to blink through.

BOTTOM No Thisbe do I see! Cursed be thy stones for thus deceiving me!

THESEUS The wall, methinks, being sensible, should curse again.

BOTTOM No, in truth sir, he should not. 'Deceiving me' is Thisbe's cue.

Enter Flute, attired as the lady Thisbe.

FLUTE O wall, full often hast thou heard my moans—

BOTTOM I see a voice; now will I to the chink, to spy and I can hear my Thisbe's face. Thisbe!

FLUTE My love!

BOTTOM Wilt thou at Ninny's tomb meet me straightway?

FLUTE Tide life, tide death, I come without delay.

They exit gracefully.

HIPPOLYTA This is the silliest stuff that ever I heard.

THESEUS The best in this kind are but shadows; and the worst are no worse, if imagination amend them.

A tomb has appeared on the stage. Flute enters cautiously, accompanied by Moonshine, in the person of Starveling with his lantern, bush and dog.

FLUTE   This is old Ninny's tomb. Where is my love?

Enter Snug, as the lion. He roars fiercely. Thisbe squeals and flies, dropping her mantle.

DEMETRIUS   Well roared, lion!

THESEUS   Well run, Thisbe!

Lion savages Thisbe's mantle, leaving it bloody, then departs.

THESEUS   Well moused, lion!

Cheers and applause, and much laughter.

Enter Bottom. He sees the bloody mantle. He exhibits wild despair.

BOTTOM   What dreadful dole is here? Eyes, do you see? How can it be?
            O dainty duck, O dear! Thy mantle good—What, stained with
            blood? O Fates, come, come! Come, tears, confound! Out
            sword, and wound the pap of Pyramus; cry that left pap, where
            heart doth hop.

He draws his sword and prepares to extinguish himself.

THESEUS   This passion would go near to make a man look sad.

HIPPOLYTA   Beshrew my heart, but I pity the man.

BOTTOM   Thus die I, thus, thus, thus. (*Stabs himself repeatedly, and falls*.) Now am I dead, now am I fled; my soul is in the sky. Moon take thy flight. (*Exit Starveling, with his lantern, bush and dog*.) Now die, die, die, die.

Bottom, with many twitches, jerks, convulsions and groans, dies. Huge applause. Bottom rises, bows in acknowledgement, and lying down, gives an encore of his death agonies. At last, and most reluctantly, he becomes still. Flute enters, and beholds the recumbent Bottom.

FLUTE   Asleep, my love? What, dead, my dove? O Pyramus, arise. Speak, speak! Quite dumb? Dead, dead? Come, trusty sword, come blade, my breast imbrue. (*After vainly attempting to wrest the sword from Bottom's death-grasp, Flute stabs himself with the scabbard*.) Thus Thisbe ends—Adieu, adieu, adieu! (*Dies*.)

THESEUS   Moonshine and Lion are left to bury the dead.

DEMETRIUS   Ay, and Wall, too.

Bottom rises.

BOTTOM   No, I assure you, the wall is down that parted their fathers. Will it please you to see the epilogue, or to hear a Bergomask dance?

THESEUS   No epilogue, I pray you; for your play needs no excuse. Never excuse. But come, your Bergomask; let your epilogue alone.

The company bow, and the dance begins. As they dance, the court begins to rise, and, still applauding, the audience drifts away. At last, Bottom and his companions are alone, and at the end of their dance. They look at one another with great satisfaction, shake hands, and depart. Now the great hall is empty and dark. A bell begins to toll midnight. There comes a glimmering of tiny lights; then Oberon, Titania, Puck and all their fairy attendants troop in, each holding up a tiny glowing lamp.

OBERON   Through the house give glimmering light . . . Sing and dance it trippingly . . .

The fairies begin to disperse, making strange patterns with their glowings.

TITANIA   Hand in hand with fairy grace, will we sing and bless this place.

OBERON
> Now, until the break of day,
> Through this house each fairy stray.
> To the best bride-bed will we,
> Which by us shall blessed be.

The fairies repeat the song as they begin to vanish into the deeper recesses of the palace.

OBERON   Trip away, make no stay; meet me all by break of day.

Oberon and Titania vanish in the wake of the vanishing lights. Puck alone remains. Then he grins and he too vanishes.

The curtain falls . . .

MACBETH

The curtain rises on a wild heath under a dark, ragged sky. Thunder and lightning. Three hideous old women, huddled together, screaming with malignant laughter.

1ST WITCH   When shall we three meet again? In thunder, lightning, or in rain?

2ND WITCH   When the hurly-burly's done, when the battle's lost and won!

1ST WITCH   Where the place?

2ND WITCH   Upon the heath!

3RD WITCH   There to meet with Macbeth!

They stare at one another, and nod.

ALL   Fair is foul and foul is fair: hover through the fog and filthy air!

Thunder and lighting. The witches vanish.

The battle is for Scotland itself. Norway has invaded. In the midst of the mad confusion of battle, the gigantic figures of Macbeth and Banquo, his companion-in-arms, lay about them with ceaseless swords. They are the great generals of Duncan, lawful king of Scotland. Presently the battle subsides. The survivors cheer and raise their swords and spears to Macbeth, the victor. He waves his sword in acknowledgement; and Banquo, taking up a drum from a fallen boy, rattles out a roll of triumph.

In the royal camp, good king Duncan learns with joy of Macbeth's victory; but at the same time, hears of the treachery of the Thane of Cawdor, who has been captured. Sadly, he shakes his head.

DUNCAN There's no art to find the mind's construction in the face. He was a gentleman on whom I built an absolute trust. Go pronounce his present death, and with his former title greet Macbeth. What he hath lost, noble Macbeth hath won.

The heath. Madman's weather! Macbeth and Banquo are on their way to the royal camp.

MACBETH So fair and foul a day I have not seen.

Suddenly they halt. Their way is barred by three hideous old women!

BANQUO   What are these, withered and so wild in their attire?

They do not answer. Banquo thumps on his drum.

BANQUO   Live you? Or are you aught that man may question?

*One by one, the witches raise their skinny fingers to their lips.
They gaze at Macbeth.*

MACBETH   Speak if you can! What are you?

1ST WITCH   All hail, Macbeth, hail to thee, Thane of Glamis!

Banquo thumps in agreement.

2ND WITCH   All hail, Macbeth, hail to thee, Thane of Cawdor!

Banquo, drumsticks raised, hesitates.

3RD WITCH   All hail, Macbeth, that shalt be king hereafter!

The drumsticks fall. Macbeth bends to pick them up.

BANQUO   If you can look into the seeds of time and say which grain will
grow, and which will not, speak then to me.

1ST WITCH   Lesser than Macbeth and greater.

2ND WITCH   Not so happy, yet much happier.

3RD WITCH   Thou shalt get kings though thou be none!

With each pronouncement, Macbeth taps humorously on Banquo's drum; but with the last, his blow is violent and splits the drumskin. The rent is in the form of a dagger! Macbeth and Banquo stare at it. As they do so, the witches vanish.

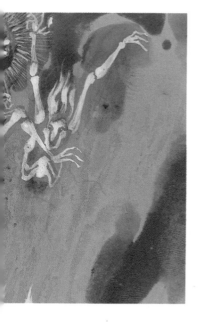

BANQUO   The earth hath bubbles, as the water has, and these are of them—

MACBETH   Your children shall be kings.

BANQUO   You shall be king—

MACBETH   —And Thane of Cawdor too; went it not so?

As they stare into the terrible air, two ghostly figures appear. As they draw near, they are seen to be two messengers from the king: Rosse and Angus. They salute Macbeth.

ROSSE   The king hath happily received, Macbeth, the news of thy success. Everyone did bear thy praises, in his kingdom's great defence, and poured them down before him. He bade me, from him, call thee Thane of Cawdor!

BANQUO   (*aside*) What! Can the Devil speak true?

MACBETH   The Thane of Cawdor lives; why do you dress me in borrowed robes?

ANGUS   Who was the Thane lives yet; but under heavy judgement bears that life which he deserves to lose.

Macbeth, in high excitement, turns aside.

MACBETH   Glamis, and Thane of Cawdor! Two truths are told, as happy prologues to the swelling act of the imperial theme! Stars, hide your fires! Let not light see my black and deep desires!

At Inverness, in the castle of Macbeth, his wife reads a letter from her husband. It tells of the meeting with the Weird Sisters and their marvellous prophecies, one of which has already come true. She puts aside the letter and paces the room.

LADY MACBETH Glamis thou art, and Cawdor, and shalt be what thou art promised.—Yet do I fear thy nature; it is too full of the milk of human kindness, to catch the nearest way. Thou wouldst be great, art not without ambition, but without the illness should attend it. Hie thee hither that I may pour my spirits in thine ear—

Comes a knocking on the door. A servant enters.

LADY MACBETH What's your tidings?

SERVANT The King comes here tonight—

LADY MACBETH Thou'rt mad to say it!

SERVANT So please you, it is true.

She dismisses the servant. She is alone. The harsh cry of a raven causes her to start. Her eyes blaze with a terrible desire.

LADY MACBETH The raven himself is hoarse that croaks the fatal entrance of Duncan under my battlements! Come, you spirits that tend on mortal thoughts, unsex me here, and fill me, from the crown to the toe, top-full of direst cruelty! Come to my woman's breasts, and take my milk for gall, you murdering ministers—

The door bursts open. Macbeth, still blood-stained from battle, stands before her.

LADY MACBETH   Great Glamis, worthy Cawdor, greater than both by the all-hail hereafter!

MACBETH   My dearest love, Duncan comes here tonight.

LACY MACBETH   And when goes hence?

MACBETH   Tomorrow, as he purposes.

LADY MACBETH   O never shall sun that morrow see! Your face, my thane, is as a book where men may read strange matters. To beguile the time look like the time, bear welcome in your eye, your hand, your tongue; look like the innocent flower, but be the serpent under't. He that's coming must be provided for; and you shall

put this night's great business into my dispatch, which shall to all our nights and days to come give solely sovereign sway and masterdom.

MACBETH   (*uncertainly*) We will speak further—

LADY MACBETH   Only look up clear; leave all the rest to me.

The courtyard of the castle. King Duncan, accompanied by his sons, Malcolm and Donalbain, and a train of nobles and servants, has arrived. Lady Macbeth greets him with loyal smiles and humble curtsies.

DUNCAN   Conduct me to mine host; we love him highly.

Evening. A banquet is in progress to honour the royal guest. The door of the dining-chamber opens briefly and a dark figure emerges. It is Macbeth. He is deeply disturbed.

MACBETH   If it were done, when 'tis done, then 'twere well it were done quickly: if the assassination could trammel up the consequence . . .? He's here in double trust; first as I am his kinsman and his subject, strong both against the deed; then as his host who should against his murderer shut the door, not bear the knife myself. Besides, this Duncan hath borne his faculties so meek, hath been so clear in his great office, that his virtues will plead like angels, trumpet-tongued, against the deep damnation of his taking-off—

The door opens and closes again. Lady Macbeth has followed him, leaving King Duncan at the banquet table.

LADY MACBETH   Why have you left the chamber?

MACBETH   We will proceed no further in this business.

LADY MACBETH   Art thou afeard to be the same in thine own act and valour as thou art in desire?

MACBETH   Prithee, peace! I dare do all that may become a man, who dares do more is none.

LADY MACBETH   What beast was't then that made you break this enterprise to me?

MACBETH If we should fail?

LADY MACBETH We fail? But screw your courage to the sticking-place and we'll not fail!

Night. The great hall of the castle. All is quiet. A flickering light appears. Macbeth, with a servant, bearing a torch. They halt.

MACBETH Go bid thy mistress, when my drink is ready, she strike upon the bell.

The servant departs, leaving the torch to glimmer on the spears and shields that hang upon the wall. Its light, reflected on the polished surfaces, seems to form the shapes of daggers . . .

MACBETH: Is this a dagger which I see before me, the handle toward my hand? . . . or art thou but a dagger of the mind . . .?

Faintly, there is the sound of a bell. Macbeth draws in his breath sharply.

MACBETH I go, and it is done: the bell invites me. Hear it not, Duncan, for it is a knell that summons thee to Heaven, or to Hell.

*Silently, he leaves the hall and begins to mount a stairway . . .
In the hall below, a softly gliding shadow appears. It is Lady
Macbeth. An owl cries.*

LADY MACBETH   Hark! Peace! It was the owl that shrieked. (*She looks up
toward the stairway, where Macbeth has vanished.*) He is
about it: the doors are open, and the surfeited grooms do mock
their charge with snores. I have drugged their possets . . . Had
he not resembled my father as he slept, I had done it.

There is a slight noise. Macbeth descends the stairs.

MACBETH   I have done the deed.

LADY MACBETH   My husband!

MACBETH   (*staring at his bloody hands*) This is a sorry sight.

LADY MACBETH   A foolish thought, to say a sorry sight. Why did you bring these
daggers from the place? They must lie there; go carry them,
and smear the sleepy grooms with blood.

MACBETH   I'll go no more. I am afraid to think what I have done; look
on't again I dare not.

LADY MACBETH   Give me the daggers! The sleeping and the dead are but as
pictures. 'Tis the eye of childhood that fears a painted devil. If
he do bleed, I'll gild the faces of the grooms withal, for it must
seem their guilt!

*She snatches the daggers and hastens away. Macbeth continues
to stare at his hands. Suddenly there is a loud knocking on the
castle's outer door.*

MACBETH   Whence is that knocking? How is't with me, when every noise
appals me? Will all great Neptune's ocean wash this blood
clean from my hand? No, this my hand will rather the
multitudinous seas incarnadine, making the green one red!

Lady Macbeth returns. She holds up her hands. They are red.

LADY MACBETH   My hands are of your colour, but I shame to wear a heart so
white.

Again, the knocking.

LADY MACBETH   Retire we to our chamber. A little water clears us of this deed. Get on your nightgown . . . Be not lost so poorly in your thoughts!

MACBETH   To know my deed, 'twere best not know myself.

For a third time, comes the knocking.

MACBETH   Wake Duncan with thy knocking: I would thou couldst!

The great door of the castle is opened. Macduff, the mighty Thane of Fife, with Lennox, a nobleman, have come to awaken the king. Macbeth, scrambled into night-attire, greets him.

MACDUFF   Is the King stirring, worthy Thane?

MACBETH   Not yet.

MACDUFF   He did bid me to call timely upon him.

MACBETH   I'll bring you to him.

He indicates the king's chamber and stands aside.

LENNOX   Goes the King hence today?

MACBETH   He does: he did appoint so.

LENNOX   The night has been unruly. Where we lay, our chimneys were
          blown down, and, as they say, lamentings heard i'the air;
          strange screams of death . . .

          Macduff rushes out of the king's chamber.

MACDUFF   Horror, horror, horror! Awake, awake! Ring the alarum bell!
          Murder and treason!

          *Uproar and terror in the castle! Banquo, the king's sons and
          Lady Macbeth appear, white-faced, amazed. Macbeth rushes
          into the king's chamber.*

LADY MACBETH   What's the business?

MACDUFF   Our royal master's murdered!

LADY MACBETH   Woe, alas! What! In our house?

Macbeth reappears. Malcolm and Donalbain, still tousled with sleep, enter.

DONALBAIN   What's amiss?

MACBETH   You are, and do not know it! The spring, the head, the fountain of your blood is stopped—

MACDUFF   Your royal father's murdered!

MALCOLM   O, by whom?

LENNOX   Those of his chamber, as it seemed, had done't. Their hands and faces were all badg'd with blood, so were their daggers—

MACBETH   O! yet do I repent me of my fury that I did kill them!

MACDUFF   Wherefore did you so?

All stare at Macbeth. Malcolm and Donalbain draw apart. They whisper fearfully.

MALCOLM   What will you do? I'll to England.

DONALBAIN   To Ireland, I. Our separated fortunes shall keep us both the safer; where we are, there's daggers in men's smiles; the near in blood, the nearer bloody.

Without a word, they vanish away like thieves in the night, leaving behind Macbeth, and the crown.

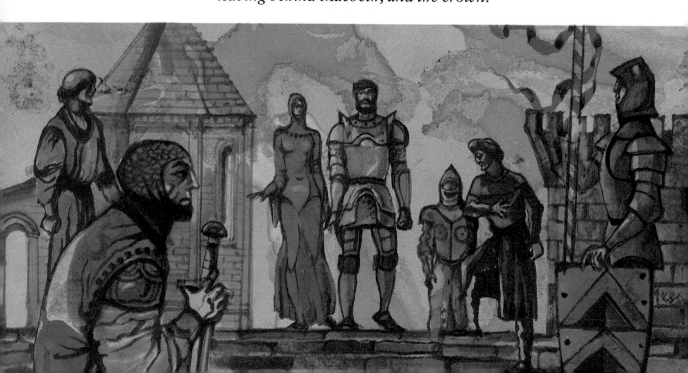

The crown of Scotland. In the great abbey church at Scone, the golden round, held in the trembling hands of a bishop, descends upon the head of Macbeth. Beside him kneels his queen. She is well satisfied. The second prophecy has been fulfilled. Yet her husband's face, far from triumphant, is bleak and haunted. He peers uneasily at the faces of the attending nobles. One, in particular, catches his eye. It is Banquo.

BANQUO (*to himself*) Thou hast it now: King, Cawdor, Glamis, all, as the weird women promised, and I fear thou played'st most foully for it; yet it was said it should not stand in thy posterity, but that myself should be the root and father of many kings . . .

A room in the royal palace. There is to be a great feast to celebrate the crowning of Macbeth. All the great ones of Scotland have been bidden to attend. Among them is Banquo, and Fleance, his son. Macbeth smiles fondly at them.

MACBETH Tonight we hold a solemn supper, sir, and I'll request your presence.

BANQUO Let your highness command upon me.

MACBETH Ride you this afternoon?

BANQUO Ay, my good lord.

MACBETH Is't far you ride?

BANQUO	As far, my lord, as will fill up the time 'twixt this and supper.
MACBETH	Goes Fleance with you?
BANQUO	Ay, my good lord.
MACBETH	Fail not our feast.
BANQUO	My lord, I will not.

Banquo and his son depart. Macbeth is alone. He goes to a window and stares out over the palace gardens.

MACBETH   To be thus is nothing, but to be safely thus. Our fears in Banquo stick deep . . .

He raises his hand. Below, two grim figures emerge from the concealment of bushes. They look up. Macbeth nods. They salute, and vanish. The door opens. Lady Macbeth enters and goes over to Macbeth.

LADY MACBETH   How now, my lord, why do you keep alone? Things without all remedy should be without regard; what's done is done.

MACBETH   We have scorched the snake, not killed it; she'll close and be herself . . . Better be with the dead, whom we, to gain our peace, have sent to peace. Duncan is in his grave; after life's fitful fever he sleeps well . . .

LADY MACBETH   You must leave this!

MACBETH   O! full of scorpions is my mind, dear wife! Thou knowest that Banquo and his Fleance lives.

LADY MACBETH   What's to be done?

MACBETH   Be innocent of the knowledge, dearest chuck, till thou applaud the deed. Come, seeling night, scarf up the tender eye of pitiful day, and with thy bloody and invisible hand cancel and tear to pieces that great bond which keeps me pale! Light thickens, and the crow makes wing to the rooky wood; good things of day begin to droop and drowse, whiles night's black agents to their prey do rouse. Thou marvel'st at my words, but hold thee still: things bad begun make strong themselves by ill.

The banqueting chamber. The flower of Scotland's nobility buzz and jostle in blossoming profusion. Sliding among them, serpent-like, Lady Macbeth darts her head from side to side, tasting the sweet air of royalty.

LADY MACBETH   You know your own degrees, sit down . . .

LORDS   Thanks to your Majesty!

They seat themselves at the great table. Music begins to play: the wild wailing of bagpipes and the rattle of a drum. A shadow lurks by the door: a muffled figure, beckoning. Macbeth observes it, and quietly approaches. The figure draws aside the covering of its face.

MACBETH   There's blood upon thy face.

MURDERER   'Tis Banquo's then.

MACBETH   Is he dispatched?

MURDERER   My lord, his throat is cut.

MACBETH   Thou art the best o' the cut-throats, yet he's good that did the like for Fleance!

MURDERER   Most royal sir, Fleance is scaped.

MACBETH   Then comes my fit again! I had else been perfect, but now I am cabined, cribbed, confined. But Banquo's safe?

MURDERER   Ay, my good lord; safe in a ditch he bides, with twenty trenched gashes on his head.

MACBETH   Thanks for that. Get thee gone.

The murderer, with a soldierly salute, vanishes away. Macbeth returns to his guests. He stares, puzzled, at the table.

LENNOX   May't please your highness, sit.

MACBETH   The table's full.

LENNOX   Here is a place reserved, sir.

MACBETH   Where?

LENNOX   Here, my good lord.

He gestures. Macbeth stares. In the offered place sits the ghost of Banquo!

MACBETH   Which of you have done this?

LORDS   What, my good lord?

The apparition raises its hand and points at Macbeth. Macbeth staggers in horror.

MACBETH   Thou canst not say I did it! Never shake thy gory locks at me!

Bewilderment at the table.

ROSSE   Gentlemen, rise, his highness is not well!

LADY MACBETH   Sit, worthy friends, my lord is often thus! Pray you keep seat! (*She goes to her husband's side, grasps him by the arm, and whispers fiercely*) Are you a man? This is the very painting of your fear! Why do you make such faces? When all's done, you look but on a stool!

MACBETH   (*pointing at the apparition*) Prithee, see there! The time has been, that when the brains were out, the man would die, and there an end; but now they rise again, with twenty mortal murders on their crowns, and push us from our stools.

The ghost vanishes. Macbeth makes an effort to recover himself. He takes up a glass of wine, and offers a toast.

MACBETH   Come, love and health to all! And to our dear friend Banquo, whom we miss! Would he were here!

He makes as if to drink. The music plays loudly; in particular, the drum. He glances at the drummer. It is Banquo! He hurls his glass at the ghost.

MACBETH   Avaunt, and quit my sight! Thy bones are marrowless, thy blood is cold; thou hast no speculation in those eyes which thou dost glare with! Hence, horrible shadow! Unreal mockery, hence!

A clatter of falling stools as everyone rises in alarm and amazement. A hubbub of voices, wondering what's amiss.

LADY MACBETH   I pray you, speak not! He grows worse and worse, question enrages him – at once, good night! Stand not upon the order of your going, but go at once!

Confusedly, the guests depart. Presently Macbeth and his wife are alone, amid the ruins of the feast.

MACBETH   It will have blood, they say: blood will have blood. What is the night?

LADY MACBETH   Almost at odds with morning, which is which.

MACBETH   How say'st thou, that Macduff denies his person at our great bidding?

LADY MACBETH   Did you send to him, sir?

MACBETH   I heard it by the way; but I will send. There's not a one of them but in his house I keep a servant fee'd. I will tomorrow to the weird sisters. More shall they speak; for I am bent to know by the worst means, the worst. I am in blood stepped in so far, that should I wade no more, returning were as tedious as going o'er.

LADY MACBETH   You lack the season of all natures, sleep.

MACBETH   Come, we'll to sleep. We are yet but young in deed.

Within a mean and smoky house, the three witches move slowly about a black cauldron that hisses and spits above a fire. As they revolve, they cast their strange offerings into the boiling pot.

1ST WITCH   Round about the cauldron go, in the poisoned entrails throw; toad that under cold stone days and nights has thirty-one.

ALL   Double, double, toil and trouble; fire burn and cauldron bubble.

2ND WITCH   Fillet of a fenny snake, in the cauldron boil and bake. Eye of newt and toe of frog, wool of bat and tongue of dog . . .

ALL   Double, double, toil and trouble; fire burn and cauldron bubble.

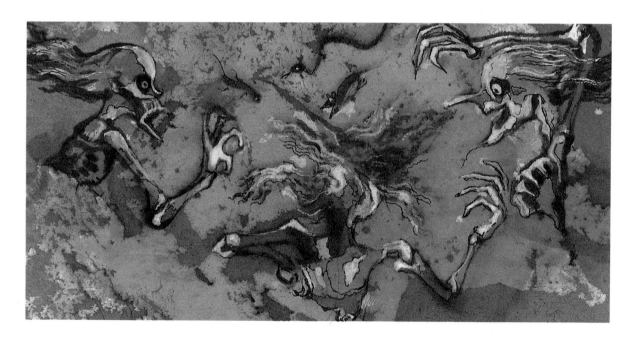

3RD WITCH   Finger of birth-strangled babe ditch-delivered by a drab, make the gruel thick and slab . . .

ALL   Double, double, toil and trouble; fire burn and cauldron bubble . . .

Comes a knocking on the door.

2ND WITCH   By the pricking of my thumbs, something wicked this way comes! Open, locks, whoever knocks!

The door opens. Macbeth enters. Vanished is the once noble warrior. His face is savage and depraved.

MACBETH   How now, you secret, black, and midnight hags? What is't you do?

ALL   A deed without a name.

MACBETH   Answer me to what I ask you.

1ST WITCH   Speak.

2ND WITCH   Demand.

3RD WITCH   We'll answer.

1ST WITCH   Say if th'hadst rather hear it from our mouths, or from our masters?

MACBETH   Call 'em; let me see 'em.

They nod. Then, from a homely jug, one of them pours blood into the cauldron. It spits in a fury. Dense vapours arise and out of the swirling air, a strange sight appears, to the accompaniment of thunder. It is a helmeted head.

1ST APPARITION Macbeth, Macbeth, Macbeth, beware Macduff, beware the Thane of Fife.

The apparition vanishes. Macbeth nods grimly.

MACBETH Thou hast harped my fear aright. But—

Thunder again. A second apparition. It is a bloody child.

2ND APPARITION Macbeth, Macbeth, Macbeth, be bloody, bold and resolute. None of woman born shall harm Macbeth.

MACBETH Then live Macduff – what need I fear of thee? But yet I'll make assurance double sure . . . thou shalt not live!

The second apparition dissolves away, and gives way, with a further, solemn roll of thunder, to a third apparition. It is a crowned child with a branch in its hand.

3RD APPARITION Macbeth shall never vanquished be until great Birnam Wood to high Dunsinane Hill shall come against him. (*It vanishes.*)

MACBETH   That will never be. Who can impress the forest, bid the tree unfix his earth-bound root? Yet my heart throbs to know one thing: shall Banquo's issue ever reign in this kingdom?

ALL   Seek to know no more.

MACBETH   I will be satisfied!

Strange music. The fire dies, the cauldron sinks into the earth.

ALL   Show his eyes, and grieve his heart; come like shadows, so depart.

Out of the thick air stalks a procession of crowned kings. There are eight of them. Last of all comes murdered, bloody Banquo. Banquo points to the kings, then to himself, and smiles. The vision and the witches disappear. Macbeth is alone.

MACBETH   Where are they? Gone? Let this pernicious hour stand aye accursed in the calendar! (*There's a knocking on the door*) Come in, without there!

Lennox enters.

MACBETH   Saw you the weird sisters?

LENNOX   No, my lord.

MACBETH   Came they not by you?

LENNOX   No indeed, my lord.

MACBETH   Infected be the air whereon they ride, and damned all those that trust them! I did hear the galloping of horse. Who was't came by?

LENNOX   'Tis two or three, my lord, that bring you word Macduff is fled to England.

MACBETH   Time, thou anticipat'st my exploits! From this moment the very firstlings of my heart shall be the firstlings of my hand! The castle of Macduff I will surprise, seize upon Fife, give to the edge of the sword his wife, his babes, and all unfortunate souls that trace him in his line. No boasting like a fool; this deed I'll do before this purpose cool.

A room in the palace. Macbeth gazes out of his murderer's window, across a wide landscape, towards a distant castle on an eminence. He raises his hand. Tiny black figures, like malignant beetles, scurry across the green land and mount the hillside towards the castle. They reach it and swarm up its walls, finding little entrances and penetrating them. On the battlements they reappear, hurling white-gowned figures to their deaths. Tiny screams reach the watcher at the window, who nods . . .

A sunlit field in peaceful England. Malcolm and Macduff stand together.

MACDUFF   Not in the legions of horrid Hell can come a devil more damned in evils to top Macbeth.

MALCOLM   Our poor country sinks beneath the yoke. Here from gracious England have I offer of goodly thousands . . .

As they talk, a horseman approaches, weary and travel-stained. It is Rosse.

MALCOLM   My ever gentle cousin, welcome hither. Stands Scotland where it did?

ROSSE   Alas, poor country! The dead man's knell is there scarce asked for who, and good men's lives expire before the flowers in their caps.

MALCOLM   What's the newest grief?

MACDUFF   How does my wife?

ROSSE   Why, well.

MACDUFF   And all my children?

ROSSE   They were well at peace when I did leave 'em.

MACDUFF   Be not a niggard of your speech. Keep it not from me; quickly, let me have it.

ROSSE   Your castle is surprised; your wife and babes savagely slaughtered –

MALCOLM   Merciful Heaven!

MACDUFF   My children too?

ROSSE   Wife, children, servants, all that could be found.

MACDUFF   My wife killed too?

ROSSE   I have said.

MACDUFF He has no children! Did you say all? – O Hell-kite! – All?
What, all my pretty chickens and their dam at one fell swoop?

MALCOLM Let grief convert to anger –

MACDUFF Front to front bring you this fiend of Scotland and myself;
within my sword's length set him!

MALCOLM Our power is ready. Macbeth is ripe for shaking . . .

*The high dark castle of Dunsinane. It is night. In a quiet
ante-chamber, a doctor and a waiting-gentlewoman stand and
murmur together.*

DOCTOR I have two nights watched with you, but can perceive no truth
in your report. When was it –

*Even as he speaks, a flickering light approaches. It is a taper,
carried by Lady Macbeth. She is in her nightgown. As she
walks, she rubs her hands together, causing the taper to tilt and
cast wild shadows.*

WOMAN Lo you, here she comes! This is her very guise, and upon my
life, fast asleep.

DOCTOR You see her eyes are open.

WOMAN Ay, but their sense are shut.

DOCTOR   What is it she does now?

WOMAN   It is an accustomed action with her, to seem thus washing her hands: I have known her continue in this for a quarter of an hour.

LADY MACBETH   Look, here's a spot.

DOCTOR   Hark, she speaks.

LADY MACBETH   Out, damned spot! out, I say! – One; two: why, 'tis time to do't. – Fie, my lord, fie! a soldier, and afeard? – What need we fear who knows it, when none can call our power to accompt? – Yet who would have thought the old man to have had so much blood in him?

DOCTOR   Do you mark that?

LADY MACBETH   The Thane of Fife had a wife: where is she now? – What, will these hands ne'er be clean?

DOCTOR   Go to, go to, you have known what you should not!

WOMAN   She has spoke what she should not: I am sure of that; Heaven knows what she has known!

LADY MACBETH   Here's the smell of the blood still. All the perfumes of Arabia will not sweeten this little hand. O, O, O!

DOCTOR   What a sigh is there! The heart is sorely charged.

WOMAN   I would not have such a heart in my bosom for the dignity of the whole body.

DOCTOR   This disease is beyond my practice –

LADY MACBETH   Wash your hands, put on your nightgown; look not so pale. I tell you yet again, Banquo's buried: he cannot come out on's grave.

DOCTOR   Even so?

LADY MACBETH   To bed, to bed: there's knocking at the gate. Come, come, come, come, give me your hand. What's done cannot be undone. To bed, to bed, to bed . . .

She drifts away.

DOCTOR   More needs she the divine than the physician. God, God forgive us all!

Open country, near Dunsinane. Two Scottish nobles on horseback meet and exchange news.

1ST NOBLE   The English power is near, led on by Malcolm and the good Macduff.

2ND NOBLE   Near Birnam Wood we shall meet them.

1ST NOBLE   What does the tyrant?

2ND NOBLE   Great Dunsinane he strongly fortifies. Some say he's mad . . .

1ST NOBLE   Now does he feel his secret murders sticking on his hands.
Those he commands move only in command, nothing in love.
Now does he feel his title hang loose about him, like a giant's
robe upon a dwarfish thief.

*Dunsinane castle. In a fierce and warlike chamber, hung with
swords and spears and shields, Macbeth, watched by the
doctor and attendants, paces to and fro in furious agitation. A
servant enters, trembling.*

MACBETH   The devil damn thee black, thou cream-faced loon! Where
got'st thou that goose-look?

SERVANT   There is ten thousand –

MACBETH   – Geese, villain?

SERVANT   Soldiers, sir. The English force –

MACBETH   – Take thy face hence! (*The servant, trembling, departs.*)

MACBETH   I am sick at heart. I have lived long enough: my way of life is
fallen into the sere, the yellow leaf, and that which should
accompany old age, as honour, love, obedience, troops of
friends, I must not look to have; but in their stead, curses, not
loud but deep, mouth-honour . . . (*He turns to the doctor.*)
How does your patient, doctor?

DOCTOR Not so sick, my lord, as she is troubled with thick-coming fancies, that keep her from her rest.

MACBETH Cure her of that: canst thou not minister to a mind diseased, pluck from the memory a rooted sorrow, raze out the written troubles of the brain, and with some sweet oblivious antidote cleanse the stuffed bosom of that perilous stuff which weighs upon the heart?

DOCTOR Therein the patient must minister to himself.

MACBETH Throw physic to the dogs; I'll none of it! (*He turns to his attendants.*) Come, put mine armour on! I'll fight till from my bones my flesh be hacked! Till Birnam Wood remove to Dunsinane, I cannot taint with fear!

The English force, led by Malcolm and Macduff, and a company of Scottish nobles. Before them stands a forest . . .

NOBLE What wood is this before us?

2ND NOBLE The Wood of Birnam.

MALCOLM Let every soldier hew him down a bough, and bear it before him.

The order is passed. The soldiers advance and, with swords and axes, cripple the trees, leaving white wounds, like dead men's faces. Presently, another forest, it seems, begins to move across the land . . .

The courtyard of Dunsinane castle. A warlike scene. Macbeth in armour, with soldiers about him. Banners fly, drums roll.

MACBETH   Hang out our banners on the outward walls!

There is a sudden cry of women from high up in the castle.

MACBETH   What is that noise?

COURTIER   It is the cry of women, my good lord. (*He goes to discover the cause.*)

MACBETH   I have almost forgot the taste of fears: the time has been, my senses would have cooled to hear a night-shriek, and my fell of hair would at a dismal treatise rise and stir as life were in it. I have supped full with horrors . . .

The courtier returns. His face is grave.

MACBETH   Wherefore was that cry?

COURTIER   The Queen, my lord, is dead.

MACBETH   She should have died hereafter; there would have been a time for such a word. Tomorrow, and tomorrow, and tomorrow creeps in this petty pace from day to day, to the last syllable of recorded time: and all our yesterdays have lighted fools the way to dusty death. Out, out brief candle! Life's but a walking shadow, a poor player that struts and frets his hour upon this stage, and then is heard no more. It is a tale told by an idiot, full of sound and fury, signifying nothing.

A soldier approaches, staring-eyed.

MACBETH   Thou com'st to use thy tongue; thy story quickly!

SOLDIER   As I did stand my watch upon the hill, I looked toward Birnam, and anon methought the wood began to move!

MACBETH   Liar and slave!

SOLDIER   Within this three mile you may see it coming; I say, a moving grove!

MACBETH   If thou speak'st false . . . (*The man shakes his head violently. Macbeth dismisses him.*) I begin to doubt the equivocation of the fiend that lies like truth. 'Fear not till Birnam Wood do come to Dunsinane,' and now a wood comes towards Dunsinane. Arm, arm, and out! If this which he avouches does appear, there is no flying hence or tarrying here. I gin to be a-weary of the sun, and wish the estate of the world were now undone. Ring the alarum bell! Blow, wind! come wrack, at least we'll die with harness on our back!

He draws his sword and, with a shout of defiance, rushes from the castle, leading his soldiers down to the forest of trees that moves inexorably towards him.

The hillside. With furious shouts, the army of Macbeth rushes down towards the ever-oncoming wood. Suddenly, the leafy boughs are flung aside, and the forces of Malcolm and Macduff are revealed. In moments, the battle is engaged. The air is full of shrieks and shouts and bitter steel, and whirling dust. Macbeth in the midst, plying his trade of war with a giant's arm and strength.

MACBETH   They have tied me to the stake; I cannot fly, but bear-like I must fight the course.

A warrior confronts him. They fight. The warrior is slain.

MACBETH   What's he that was not born of woman? Such a one am I to fear, or none!

On another part of the hill, Macduff seeks Macbeth.

MACDUFF   That way the noise is. Tyrant, show thy face. If thou be'st slain, and with no stroke of mine, my wife and children's ghosts will haunt me still. I cannot strike at wretched kerns, whose arms are hired to bear their staves. Either thou, Macbeth, or else my sword with an unbattered edge I sheathe again undeeded. There thou shouldst be: by this great clatter one of greatest note seems bruited. Let me find him, fortune! and more I beg not.

He sees Macbeth.

MACDUFF   Turn, hell-hound, turn!

MACBETH   (*turning*) Of all men else I have avoided thee. But get thee back! My soul is too much charged with blood of thine already!

MACDUFF   I have no words; my voice is in my sword, thou bloodier villain than terms can give thee out.

They fight.

MACBETH   Thou losest labour. I bear a charmed life, which must not yield to one of woman born!

MACDUFF   Despair thy charm, and let the Angel whom thou still hast served, tell thee, Macduff was from his mother's womb untimely ripped!

MACBETH   Accursed be that tongue that tells me so, for it hath cowed my better part of man! And be these juggling fiends no more believed, that palter with us in a double sense, that keep the word of promise to our ear, and break it to our hope. I'll not fight with thee.

MACDUFF   Then yield thee, coward; and live to be the show and gaze o'the time. We'll have thee, as our rarer monsters are, painted upon a pole, and underwrit, 'Here may you see the tyrant.'

MACBETH   I will not yield. Though Birnam Wood be come to Dunsinane, and thou opposed, being of no woman born, yet will I try the last! Before my body I throw my warlike shield: lay on, Macduff, and damned be him that first cries, 'Hold, enough!'

They fight, and vanish into the clouds of dust, fighting. Suddenly there is a cry of dismay. The air thins and the head of Macbeth rises up, fierce and unrepentant. But the head is all. It has been severed at the neck, and is fixed upon the sword of Macduff.

There is a mighty shout of joy. Macbeth is dead: the battle has been lost and won.

The curtain falls . . .

THE TEMPEST

The curtain rises on Prospero's isle, a strange, uninhabited place, mysterious with mists, and set in the midst of a glassy sea. The lord of the isle, clad in his magic mantle, stands upon a promontory with his arm about his daughter, Miranda. Together, they gaze out towards a distant ship. Prospero's eyes are glittering.

At last, after twelve long years on the haunted isle, his enemies are within his grasp: his wicked brother Antonio, Alonso, the greedy King of Naples, and his treacherous brother Sebastian; even Gonzalo, the kindly courtier who, when he and his tiny daughter had been set adrift in a rotting boat, had secretly provided them with food and clothing, and those precious books from his library that had turned the poor, betrayed Duke of Milan into Prospero, the mighty enchanter.

He raises the carved staff he holds in his right hand, and stretches out towards the distant ship. At once, a black cloud appears in the clear sky. It assumes a wild and savage shape, and pounces on the vessel. It is full of dazzling worms of lightning, and the vessel heaves and twists in a vain effort to escape. Tiny shouts and screams reach the silent onlookers.

VOICES We split, we split!

A VOICE Hell is empty and all the devils are here!

The ship's company leap overboard; then the black cloud obscures all. When it has dispersed, the sea is glassy again. The vessel has vanished.

MIRANDA Poor souls, they perished!

PROSPERO Be collected: no more amazement: tell your piteous heart there's no harm done.

MIRANDA O, woe the day!

PROSPERO No harm. I have done nothing but in care of thee.

He seats himself; she sits beside him. Fondly, he strokes her hair, then gently touches her eyes.

PROSPERO Thou art inclined to sleep.

Miranda sleeps. Prospero rises and paces the sands.

PROSPERO Come away, servant come. I am ready now. Approach, my Ariel, come!

A strange creature manifests itself out of the air, a bright, trembling, vague creature, neither beast nor human, but endlessly changing between them.

ARIEL All hail, great master! Grave sir, hail!

PROSPERO Hast thou, spirit, performed to point the tempest that I bade thee?

ARIEL (*proudly*) To every article! I boarded the King's ship, now on the beak, now in the waist, in every cabin, I flamed amazement!

PROSPERO My brave spirit!

ARIEL Not a soul but felt a fever of the mad, and played some tricks of desperation!

PROSPERO	But are they, Ariel, safe?
ARIEL	Not a hair perished! In troops I have dispersed them 'bout the isle. The King's son I have landed by himself.
PROSPERO	Why, that's my spirit! But there's more work—
ARIEL	What, more toil?
PROSPERO	How now? Moody? What is't thou canst demand?
ARIEL	My liberty.
PROSPERO	Before the time be out? No more! Dost thou forget from what a torment I did free thee?
ARIEL	Pardon, master, I will be correspondent to command and do my spiriting gently.
PROSPERO	Do so; and after two days I will discharge thee.

ARIEL   That's my noble master! What shall I do? say what? what shall I do?

PROSPERO   Go make thyself like a nymph o'the sea, be subject to no sight but thine and mine, invisible to every eyeball else. (*Instantly, Ariel, with a flurry of strange gestures, becomes a sea-nymph, lovely and delicate.*) Fine apparition! My quaint Ariel, hark in thine ear. (*He whispers in Ariel's ear*).

ARIEL   My lord, it shall be done. (*He vanishes.*)

Prospero returns to the sleeping Miranda.

PROSPERO   Awake, dear heart, awake! Thou hast slept well. (*Miranda wakes.*) Come on, we'll visit Caliban, my slave—

MIRANDA   'Tis a villain, sir, I do not love to look on.

PROSPERO   But as 'tis we cannot miss him: he does make our fire, fetch in our wood. (*Together, they walk to the entrance of a cave.*) What, ho! Slave! Caliban! Thou earth, thou! Come forth!

With much groaning, Caliban, a monstrous, deformed creature, crawls out.

CALIBAN   A south-west blow on ye and blister you all o'er!

PROSPERO   For this, be sure, tonight thou shalt have cramps, side-stitches that shall pen thy breath up—

CALIBAN   I must eat my dinner. This island's mine, by Sycorax my
            mother, which thou tak'st from me. When thou cam'st first,
            thou strok'st me and made much of me, would'st give me
            water with berries in't, and teach me how to name the bigger
            light, and how the less, that burn by day and night; and then I
            loved thee—

PROSPERO   Thou most lying slave, whom stripes may move, not kindness!
            I have used thee, filth as thou art, with human care; and lodged
            thee in mine own cell, till thou didst seek to violate the honour
            of my child.

CALIBAN   O, ho, O, ho! Would't had been done! Thou did'st prevent me;
            I had peopled else this isle with Calibans!

PROSPERO   Hag-seed, hence! Fetch us in fuel!

CALIBAN   (creeping away) I must obey. His art is of such power . . .

            *Another part of the island. The sea-shore. Ferdinand, the
            king's son, saved from the sea, walks warily. The invisible Ariel
            leads him with a song:*

ARIEL   Come unto these yellow sands,
                        And then take hands:
                        Curtsied when you have, and kissed,
                        The wild waves whist . . .

FERDINAND	Where should this music be? I'th'air or th'earth?
ARIEL	Full fathom five thy father lies;
	Of his bones are coral made;
	Those are pearls that were his eyes:
	Nothing of him that doth fade,
	But doth suffer a sea-change
	Into something rich and strange . . .
FERDINAND	The ditty does remember my drowned father.

Little by little, the singing, invisible Ariel leads Ferdinand into the presence of Prospero and Miranda.

MIRANDA	What is't? A spirit?
PROSPERO	No, wench; it eats and sleeps and has such senses as we have—such. This gallant which thou seest was in the wreck. He hath lost his fellows and strays about to find 'em.
MIRANDA	I might call him a thing divine; for nothing natural I ever saw so noble!

Even as Miranda stares in wonderment at Ferdinand, so does he stare at the girl.

| FERDINAND | Most sure the goddess on whom these airs attend! O you wonder! If you be maid or no? |

MIRANDA	No wonder, sir; but certainly a maid.
FERDINAND	My language! heavens! I am the best of them that speak this speech, were I but where 'tis spoken.
PROSPERO	(*aside*) At first sight they have changed eyes! Delicate Ariel, I'll set thee free for this! (*To Ferdinand*) How? the best? What wert thou, if the King of Naples heard thee? A word, good sir, I fear you have done yourself some wrong: a word.
MIRANDA	Why speaks my father so ungently? This is the third man that e'er I saw; the first that e'er I sighed for—
FERDINAND	O, if a virgin, and your affection not gone forth, I'll make you the Queen of Naples!
PROSPERO	I charge thee: thou dost here usurp the name thou ow'st not; and hast put thyself upon this island as a spy, to win it from me, the lord on't.
FERDINAND	No, as I am a man!
PROSPERO	(*Miranda moves to defend Ferdinand*) Speak not you for him: he's a traitor. Come, I'll manacle thy neck and feet together—
FERDINAND	No; I will resist—

He draws his sword. Prospero raises his staff, and Ferdinand finds his arm frozen. Desperately, Miranda clutches at her father's mantle.

PROSPERO	Hence! Hang not on my garments!
MIRANDA	Sir, have pity! I'll be his surety!
PROSPERO	What! An advocate for an impostor! Hush! Thou thinkest there is no more shapes such as he, having seen but him and Caliban: foolish wench! To th'most of men this is a Caliban, and they to him are angels.
MIRANDA	My affections are most humble; I have no ambition to see a goodlier man.
PROSPERO	(*to Ferdinand*) Come on, obey!
MIRANDA	Be of comfort; my father's of a better nature, sir, than he appears . . .
PROSPERO	(*aside to Ariel, who has been hovering, invisible*) Thou shalt be as free as mountain winds; but then exactly do all points of my command . . .

A woodland glade, in which the chief survivors of the wreck now find themselves; Alonso, King of Naples; Sebastian, his brother; Antonio, brother to Prospero; Gonzalo, the kindly courtier who had once assisted Prospero and his daughter; and other attending lords. They are plainly weary from walking.

GONZALO	Beseech you, sir, be merry; you have cause, so have we all, of joy; for our escape is much beyond our loss—

ALONSO   Prithee, peace.

SEBASTIAN   (*to Antonio*) He receives comfort like cold porridge.

GONZALO   The air breathes upon us here most sweetly—

SEBASTIAN   As if it had lungs, and rotten ones.

GONZALO   Our garments, being as they were, drenched in the sea, seem now as fresh as when we were at Tunis at the marriage of your daughter who is now Queen.

ALONSO   Would I had never married my daughter there! For, coming thence, my son is lost. O thou mine heir of Naples and Milan, what strange fish hath made his meal on thee?

GONZALO   Sir, he may live; I saw him beat the surges under him—

ALONSO   No, no, he's gone.

SEBASTIAN   Sir, you may thank yourself for this great loss, that would not bless our Europe with your daughter—

ALONSO   Prithee, peace.

SEBASTIAN   The fault's your own!

GONZALO   My lord Sebastian, the truth you speak doth lack some gentleness. You rub the sore when you should bring the plaster.

Ariel appears above, hovering invisibly; and makes strange signs in the air. Gonzalo, the king and the attendant lords become suddenly drowsy. They settle on the ground.

GONZALO   You are . . . gentlemen of—of . . . I am very heavy.

ANTONIO   Go sleep. (*Gonzalo sleeps.*)

ALONSO   I wish mine eyes would, with themselves, shut my thoughts . . . (*He yawns.*) I find they are inclined to do so.

The king sleeps, and following his example so do all, except for Sebastian and Antonio.

SEBASTIAN   What a strange drowsiness possesses them!

ANTONIO   It is the quality o'th'climate.

SEBASTIAN   I find not myself disposed to sleep.

ANTONIO   Nor I.

Antonio glances at the sleeping king, and then looks meaningly at Sebastian.

ANTONIO   What might, worthy Sebastian?—O what might? My strong imagination sees a crown dropping upon thy head.

SEBASTIAN   Prithee, say on.

ANTONIO   Will you grant with me that Ferdinand is drowned?

SEBASTIAN   He's gone.

ANTONIO   Then tell me, who's the next heir to Naples?

SEBASTIAN   Claribel.

ANTONIO   She that is Queen of Tunis; she that dwells ten leagues beyond man's life. (*He nods towards the sleeping king.*) What a sleep were this for your advancement! Do you understand me?

SEBASTIAN   Methinks I do. I remember you did supplant your brother Prospero.

ANTONIO   True: and look how well my garments sit upon me.

SEBASTIAN   Thy case, dear friend, shall be my precedent; as thou got'st Milan, I'll come by Naples. Draw thy sword!

The friends creep upon the sleepers with drawn swords, ready to murder the king and Gonzalo. Swiftly, Ariel descends.

ARIEL   (*in Gonzalo's ear*)Awake, awake!

The sleepers awake, and see Sebastian and Antonio with drawn swords.

ALONSO   Why, how now? Why are you drawn?

GONZALO   What's the matter?

SEBASTIAN   We heard a hollow burst of bellowing, like bulls, or rather lions!

ALONSO   I heard nothing.

ANTONIO   Sure, it was a roar of a whole herd of lions!

ALONSO   Heard you this, Gonzalo?

GONZALO   Upon mine honour, sir, I heard a humming – there was a noise, that's verily.

ALONSO   Lead off this ground; and let's make further search for my poor son.

They all rise and leave the glade, watched by Ariel.

Another part of the island. Enter Caliban, bearing heavy logs for firewood on his back.

CALIBAN   All the infections that the sun sucks up from bogs, fens, flats, on Prosper fall, and make him by inch-meal, a disease . . .

Trinculo, the king's jester, who has also escaped the wreck enters. In his clown's motley, he presents a strange sight.

CALIBAN   Lo, now lo! Here comes a spirit of his, and to torment me for bringing wood in slowly. I'll fall flat; perchance he will not mind me!

Caliban falls flat, and covers himself with his rough cloak. He lies motionless. Trinculo stumbles over him. Cautiously he investigates.

TRINCULO   What have we here? A man or a fish? Dead or alive? A fish: he smells like a fish; a very ancient and fish-like smell. (*He feels under the cloak.*) Warm, o'my troth! This is no fish, but an islander, who hath lately suffered by a thunder-bolt!

There is a loud peal of thunder.

Alas, the storm is come again! My best way is to creep under his gaberdine; there is no other shelter hereabout: misery acquaints a man with strange bed-fellows!

He creeps under the cloak and settles down, so that his legs and Caliban's protrude at opposite ends. Now comes yet another survivor. It is Stephano, the king's butler. As always he is clutching a bottle and is drunk. He sings.

STEPHANO

> I shall no more to sea, to sea
> Here shall I die ashore . . .

This is a very scurvy tune to sing at a man's funeral; here's my comfort!

He drinks, and kicks accidentally against the combined Caliban–Trinculo.

CALIBAN   Do not torment me—O!

Stephano investigates the four-legged cloak.

STEPHANO   This is some monster of the isle with four legs, who hath got, as I take it, an ague. Where the devil should he learn our language?

CALIBAN   Do not torment me, prithee; I'll bring my wood home faster.

STEPHANO   He is in his fit now, and does not talk after the wisest. He shall taste of my bottle. Come on your ways; open your mouth—

He thrusts the bottle under the cloak, and there is a noise of gulping.

TRINCULO   I should know that voice: it should be—but he is drowned!

STEPHANO   Four legs and two voices! Amen! I will pour some in thy other mouth!

TRINCULO   Stephano! If thou beest Stephano, touch me, and speak to me; for I am Trinculo!

STEPHANO   If thou beest Trinculo, come forth!

Trinculo comes forth. He and Stephano stare at one another; and then, in an access of joy, Trinculo seizes Stephano and whirls him round in a dance.

TRINCULO   O Stephano, two Neapolitans 'scaped!

STEPHANO   Prithee, do not turn me about; my stomach is not constant.

CALIBAN   (*emerging*) That's a brave god, and bears celestial liquor. I will kneel to him.

STEPHANO   How didst thou 'scape? I escaped upon a butt of sack, which the sailors heaved o'erboard.

TRINCULO   O Stephano, hast any more of this?

STEPHANO   The whole butt, man.

CALIBAN   Hast thou not dropped from heaven?

The two friends, as if for the first time, see Caliban kneeling.

STEPHANO   Out o'the moon, I do assure thee. I was the man i'the moon . . .

CALIBAN   I have seen thee in her, and I do adore thee!

STEPHANO   Come, swear to that; kiss the book. (*He proffers the bottle.*)

TRINCULO   This is a very shallow monster! The man i'th'moon! A most poor credulous monster!

CALIBAN   I will kiss thy foot; I prithee, be my god.

TRINCULO   I shall laugh myself to death at this puppy-headed monster! I could find in my heart to beat him—

STEPHANO   Come, kiss!

TRINCULO   —but that the poor monster's in drink!

CALIBAN   (*rising*) I'll show thee the best springs; I'll pluck thee berries; I'll fish for thee, and get thee wood enough. A plague upon the tyrant that I serve!

TRINCULO   A most ridiculous monster, to make a wonder of a poor drunkard!

STEPHANO   I prithee now, lead the way. Trinculo, the King and all our company else being drowned, we will inherit here!

Caliban takes up his burden of logs, and staggering drunkenly, leads the way and sings as he goes:

CALIBAN
> 'Ban, 'Ban, Cacaliban,
> Has a new master:—get a new man!
> Freedom, high-day! high-day, freedom!
> Freedom, high-day, freedom!

Before Prospero's cell. Ferdinand, a prisoner, staggers under the weight of a log that he bears from one pile to another. As he toils, Miranda slips out of the cell.

MIRANDA   Alas now, pray you, work not so hard. My father is hard at study; pray, now, rest yourself. He's safe for these three hours.

Prospero watches Miranda and Ferdinand from concealment. He smiles to himself.

PROSPERO   Poor worm, thou art infected.

MIRANDA   You look wearily.

FERDINAND   No, noble mistress: 'tis fresh morning with me when you are by at night. What is your name?

MIRANDA   Miranda.

FERDINAND   Admired Miranda! Indeed the top of admiration! Hear my soul speak: the very instant that I saw you, did my heart fly to your service!

MIRANDA   Do you love me?

FERDINAND   O heaven, O earth, bear witness! I, beyond all limit of what else i'th'world, do love, prize, honour you!

MIRANDA   I am a fool to weep at what I am glad of.

PROSPERO   Fair encounter of two most rare affections! Heavens rain grace on that which breeds between 'em!

FERDINAND   Wherefore weep you?

MIRANDA   At mine unworthiness, that dare not offer what I desire to give. I am your wife if you will marry me; if not, I'll die your maid.

FERDINAND   My mistress, dearest—

MIRANDA   My husband, then?

FERDINAND   Ay, with a heart as willing as bondage e'er of freedom. Here's my hand.

MIRANDA   And mine, with my heart in't. And now farewell till half an hour hence.

A forest clearing, in which Stephano has laid up his wine barrel. King-like, he sits upon it. Trinculo stands beside him, and Caliban lays his burden of firewood at his new master's feet. Stephano holds out his bottle.

STEPHANO   Servant-monster, drink to me!

TRINCULO   Servant-monster! The folly of this island! They say there's but five upon this isle: we are three of them; if th'other two be brain'd like us, the state totters.

CALIBAN   (*drinking*) How does thy honour? Let me lick thy shoe. I'll not serve him, he is not valiant.

TRINCULO   Thou liest, most ignorant monster!

STEPHANO   Trinculo, keep a good tongue in your head: if you prove a mutineer,—the next tree!

CALIBAN   I thank my noble lord. As I told thee before, I am subject to a tyrant, a sorcerer, that by his cunning hath cheated me of the island.

Ariel, as ever, invisible to all, appears and stands behind Trinculo.

ARIEL   (*in Trinculo's voice*) Thou liest!

CALIBAN   Thou liest, thou jesting monkey, thou! I would my valiant master would destroy thee, I do not lie.

STEPHANO   Trinculo, if you trouble him any more in's tale, by this hand, I will supplant some of your teeth!

TRINCULO   Why, I said nothing.

CALIBAN   I say, by sorcery he got this isle; from me he got it. If thy greatness will revenge it on him, thou shalt be lord of it, and I'll serve thee.

STEPHANO   How now shall this be compassed?

CALIBAN   I'll yield him to thee asleep, where thou mayst knock a nail into his head.

ARIEL   (*in Trinculo's voice*) Thou liest: thou canst not.

CALIBAN   What a pied ninny's this! Thou scurvy patch!

TRINCULO   Why, what did I? I did nothing.

ARIEL   (*in Trinculo's voice*) Thou liest.

STEPHANO   Take thou that! (*He beats Trinculo furiously. Trinculo retires in tears. Caliban claps his hands in delight.*) Now, forward with your tale.

CALIBAN   'Tis a custom with him in the afternoon to sleep: there thou mayst brain him having first seized his books. Remember, first to possess his books; for without them he's but a sot, as I am. Burn but his books. And that most deeply to consider is the beauty of his daughter; he himself calls her a nonpareil.

STEPHANO   Is it so brave a lass?

CALIBAN   Ay, lord, she will become thy bed, I warrant, and bring thee forth brave brood.

STEPHANO   Monster, I will kill this man: his daughter and I will be king and queen—save our graces!—and Trinculo and thyself shall be viceroys. Dost thou like the plot, Trinculo?

TRINCULO   Excellent!

STEPHANO   Give me thy hand, I am sorry I beat thee; but while thou liv'st, keep a good tongue in thy head.

CALIBAN   Within this half hour he will be asleep. Wilt thou destroy him then?

ARIEL   This will I tell my master. (*Ariel plays strange music.*)

TRINCULO   (*frightened*) O forgive me my sins!

STEPHANO   (*boldly*) He that dies pays all debts. I defy thee. Mercy upon us!

He strikes at the air, wildly, as the music seems to taunt them.

CALIBAN   Be not afeared; the isle is full of noises, sounds and sweet airs, that give delight and hurt not. Sometimes a thousand twangling instruments will hum about mine ears; and sometimes voices, that if I then had waked after long sleep, will make me sleep again, and then in dreaming, the clouds methought would open, and show riches ready to drop upon me, that when I waked, I cried to dream again.

STEPHANO   This will prove a brave kingdom to me, where I shall have my music for nothing.

CALIBAN   When Prospero is destroyed.

Another part of the island. The king and his followers are walking wearily through a wood.

GONZALO   By'r lakin, I can go no further, sir; my old bones ache.

ALONSO   Old lord, I cannot blame thee. Sit down and rest.

The king, Gonzalo and the attendant lords sit; Sebastian and Antonio draw apart.

SEBASTIAN   (*touching his sword*) The next advantage will we take thoroughly.

ANTONIO   Let it be tonight.

A strange, solemn music fills the air.

ANTONIO   What harmony is this?

GONZALO   Marvellous sweet music!

From concealment, Prospero watches his enemies. He raises his staff. Strange shapes, with beast and bird heads, appear, bearing a rich banquet. They set it down before the amazed company, bow, and vanish as suddenly as they had come.

ALONSO   Give us kind keepers, heavens! What were these?

SEBASTIAN   A living drollery.

GONZALO   If in Naples I should report this now, would they believe me?

ALONSO   I cannot too much muse such shapes, such gesture, and such sound expressing (although they want the use of tongue) a kind of excellent dumb discourse.

PROSPERO   (*to the apparitions*) Praise in departing.

GONZALO   They vanished strangely.

SEBASTIAN   No matter, since they have left their viands behind. Will't please you taste of what is here?

As they advance towards the table, there is thunder and lightning. The air darkens, and with a thudding of leathery wings, Ariel, in the form of a harpy, a hideous bird with the head of a hag, flies down and perches on the table. Prospero's enemies look on in astonishment when, at a clap of the bird's wings, the banquet vanishes.

ARIEL   (*screaming*) You are three men of sin—

All draw their swords and advance upon the apparition.

ARIEL   You fools! I and my fellows are ministers of Fate. Your swords are now too massy for your strengths.

Swords fall from helpless hands. The king and his company are motionless, spellbound.

ARIEL   You three from Milan did supplant good Prospero: exposed unto the sea him and his innocent child; for which foul deed the powers, delaying, not forgetting, have incensed the seas and shores, yea, all the creatures, against your peace. Thee of thy son, Alonso, they have bereft; and do pronounce by me ling'ring perdition . . .

Thunder and lightning; and Ariel vanishes.

ALONSO O, it is monstrous, monstrous! Methought the billows spoke, and told me it, the winds did sing it to me, and the thunder, that deep and dreadful organ-pipe, pronounced the name of Prosper: therefore my son i'th'ooze is bedded; and I'll seek him deeper than e'er plummet sounded, and with him there lie mudded . . .

Before Prospero's cell, Ferdinand and Miranda together. Prospero smiles upon them. His harshness towards Ferdinand has vanished.

PROSPERO If I have too austerely punished you, your compensation makes amends. All thy vexations were but my trials of thy love, and thou hast strangely stood the test. Here, afore heaven, I ratify this, my rich gift. (*He gives Ferdinand Miranda's willing hand.*)

FERDINAND I do believe it, against an oracle.

PROSPERO Then, as my gift, and thine own acquisition, worthily purchased, take my daughter. Sit then and talk with her, she is thine own.

Prospero leaves the lovers to converse while he moves aside.

PROSPERO What Ariel! my industrious servant, Ariel!

ARIEL (*appearing*) What would my potent master?

PROSPERO   Go bring the rabble (o'er whom I give thee power) here to this place. Incite them to quick motion, for I must bestow upon the eyes of this young couple some vanity of mine art. It is my promise, and they expect it from me. (*Ariel departs on Prospero's errand. Prospero returns to Ferdinand and Miranda, who are embracing. Prospero shakes his head warningly.*)

PROSPERO   Do not give dalliance too much the rein.

FERDINAND   (*guiltily freeing Miranda*) I warrant you, sir—

PROSPERO   —No tongue! all eyes! Be silent!

Prospero raises his staff. Music plays and the air grows strangely bright, and full of swirling shapes. Iris, goddess of the rainbow appears, and, bowing, ushers in two goddesses more: Ceres, goddess of the harvest, and Juno, the queen of heaven.

JUNO   Honour, riches, marriage-blessing,
Long continuance and increasing,
Hourly joys be still upon you,
Juno sings her blessings on you.

CERES   Earth's increase, foison plenty,
Barns and garners never empty,
Scarcity and want shall shun you,
Ceres' blessing so is on you.

FERDINAND   (*awed*) This is a most majestic vision! May I be bold to think these spirits?

PROSPERO   Spirits which, by mine art, I have from their confines called to enact my present fancies.

More spirits appear, and dance gracefully.

FERDINAND   Let me live here ever! So rare a wondered father and a wise makes this place Paradise.

Prospero smiles. Suddenly his brow darkens.

PROSPERO   I had forgot that foul conspiracy of Caliban and his confederates against my life. The minute of their plot is almost come. Well done! Avoid! No more!

He gestures with his staff. The music jangles into discord and the spirits that have presented the marvellous vision fly, as if in terror. Ferdinand and Miranda look frightened.

PROSPERO   You do look, my son, in a moved sort, as if you were dismayed; be cheerful, sir. Our revels now are ended. These our actors (as I foretold you) were all spirits, and are melted into air, into thin air, and like the baseless fabric of this vision, the cloud clapped towers, the gorgeous palaces, the solemn

temples, the great globe itself, yea, all which it inherit, shall dissolve, and like this insubstantial pageant faded leave not a rack behind. We are such stuff as dreams are made on; and our little life is rounded with a sleep. Sir, I am vexed; bear with my weakness. If you be pleased, retire into my cell. A turn or two I'll walk to still my beating mind.

The lovers retire into Prospero's cell.

PROSPERO   Ariel, come!

ARIEL   (*appearing*) What's thy pleasure?

PROSPERO   Spirit, we must prepare to meet with Caliban. Where didst thou leave these varlots?

ARIEL   They were red-hot with drinking, so full of valour that they smote the air for breathing in their faces! I left them i'th'filthy-mantled pool beyond your cell, there dancing up to th'chins, that the foul lake o'erstunk their feet!

PROSPERO   This was well done, my bird. The trumpery in my house, go bring it hither, for stale to catch these thieves! (*Ariel departs.*) I will plague them all, even to roaring.

Ariel returns, bearing a host of rich garments, which, on Prospero's direction, are hung on a line close by the entrance to his cell. Then Prospero and Ariel conceal themselves. Even as they do so, the conspirators enter: Caliban, Stephano and Trinculo. They are soaked with filthy water.

CALIBAN	Pray you tread softly; we now are near his cell.
TRINCULO	Monster, I do smell all horse-piss, at which my nose is in great indignation.
STEPHANO	So is mine. Do you hear, monster?
CALIBAN	Prithee, my king, be quiet. Seest thou here, this is the mouth o'th'cell. No noise, and enter.
STEPHANO	Give me thy hand. I do begin to have bloody thoughts.

Suddenly Trinculo sees the garments on the line.

TRINCULO	O King Stephano! Look what a wardrobe is here for thee!

THE TEMPEST

At once, the two drunkards busy themselves with all the fine clothing.

CALIBAN   Let it alone, thou fool, it is but trash!

STEPHANO   (*covetously*) Put off that gown, Trinculo. By this hand, I'll have that gown!

He tears the coveted garment off Trinculo.

CALIBAN   Let it alone, and do the murder first!

STEPHANO   Monster, go to, carry this!

He thrusts an armful of garments on Caliban.

TRINCULO   And this. (*More garments.*)

STEPHANO   Ay, and this!

Prospero raises his staff. At once, there is a sound of hunting horns, and out of the wood come huge, savage hounds, baying and barking. The would-be murderers howl in terror and dismay. They fly from the hounds. Prospero and Ariel urge the hunt on.

PROSPERO   Hey, Mountain, hey!

ARIEL   Silver! There goes Silver!

PROSPERO   Fury, Fury! There, Tyrant there! Hark, hark!

The sounds of barking and the howls of the pursued die away.

PROSPERO   Say, my spirit, how fares the King and's followers?

ARIEL   Just as you left them—all prisoners, sir. They cannot budge till your release. Your charm so strongly works 'em that if you now beheld them your affections would become tender.

PROSPERO   Dost think so, spirit?

ARIEL   Mine would, sir, were I human.

PROSPERO   And mine shall. The rarer action is in virtue than in vengeance. Go release them, Ariel.

Ariel departs. Prospero draws a circle on the ground with his staff. Sadly, he shakes his head.

PROSPERO   This rough magic I here abjure; and when I have required some heavenly music (which even now I do) to work mine end upon their senses that this airy charm is for, I'll break my staff, bury it certain fathoms in the earth, and deeper than did ever plummet sound I'll drown my book.

There is solemn music; Ariel leads the spellbound king and his followers into Prospero's magic circle, and leaves them, stiff and doll-like. Prospero now takes off his magic mantle and reveals the stately dress of the Duke of Milan. He waves his staff. The spell is lifted, and the prisoners blink in amazement.

PROSPERO   Behold, sir King, the wronged Duke of Milan, Prospero.

Alonso falls to his knees.

ALONSO   Thy dukedom I resign, and do entreat thou pardon me my
            wrongs. But how should Prospero be living, and be here?

PROSPERO   (*to Gonzalo*) First, noble friend, let me embrace thine age,
            whose honour cannot be measured or confined.

GONZALO   Whether this be, or be not, I'll not swear.

PROSPERO   You do yet taste some subtleties o' the isle, that will not let you
            believe things certain. Welcome, my friends all! (*He turns to
            Sebastian and Antonio.*) But you, my brace of lords, were I so
            minded, I here could pluck his Highness' frown upon you and
            justify you traitors. At this time I will tell no tales.

SEBASTIAN   (*aside*) The devil speaks in him!

PROSPERO   No. For you, most wicked sir, whom to call brother would
            even infect my mouth, I do forgive thy rankest fault—all of
            them; and require my dukedom of thee, which perforce, I
            know thou must restore.

*Antonio scowls and shrugs his shoulders. He turns away.
Prospero addresses the king.*

PROSPERO   This cell's my court. Pray you, look in. My dukedom since
            you have given me again, I will requite you with as good a thing.

*They approach the entrance to the cell. Prospero draws aside a
curtain, and reveals Ferdinand and Miranda, playing chess.*

MIRANDA	Sweet lord, you play me false.
FERDINAND	No, my dearest love, I would not for the world.
MIRANDA	Yes, for a score of kingdoms you should wrangle, and I would call it fair play—

The lovers, seeing they are observed, break off. Ferdinand runs to kneel at his father's feet.

FERDINAND	Though the seas threaten, they are merciful. I have cursed them without cause!
ALONSO	(*embracing him*) All the blessings of a glad father compass thee about!
MIRANDA	O, wonder! How many goodly creatures are there here! How beauteous mankind is! O brave new world, that has such people in it!
PROSPERO	'Tis new to thee.

ALONSO	Who is this maid with whom thou wast at play? Is she the goddess that hath severed us, and brought us together?
FERDINAND	Sir, she is mortal; but by immortal Providence she's mine. She is daughter to this famous Duke of Milan.

The king warmly embraces his son and his son's bride. Ariel enters, leading the ship's master and the boatswain, both in a state of dreamlike wonderment.

GONZALO	O look sir, look sir, here is more of us! What is the news?
BOATSWAIN	The best news is that we have safely found our king and company; the next, our ship—which but three glasses since, we gave out split—is tight and yare and bravely rigged as when we first put out to sea!
ARIEL	(*aside to Prospero*) Was't well done?
PROSPERO	Bravely, my diligence. Thou shalt be free. (*Ariel soars into the air and disappears.*)
ALONSO	This is as strange a maze as e'er men trod—

PROSPERO   There are yet missing of your company some few odd lads that you remember not. (*Ariel returns, driving a woeful Caliban and the reeling, drunken, tattered Stephano and Trinculo.*) Two of these fellows you must know and own. This thing of darkness I acknowledge mine. (*He turns to Caliban.*) Go, sirrah, to my cell. As you look to have my pardon, trim it handsomely.

CALIBAN   Ay, that I will; and I'll be wise hereafter, and seek for grace. What a thrice double ass was I to take this drunkard for a god, and worship this dull fool!

The three would-be lords of the isle stumble away to nurse their bruises and ease their cramps.

ALONSO   I long to hear the story of your life, which must take the ear strangely.

PROSPERO   I'll deliver all, and promise you calm seas . . . (*To Ariel, aside*) My Ariel, chick, that is thy charge. Then to the elements be free, and fare thou well.

Prospero raises his hand in farewell. Then, with a courteous gesture, he conducts the company into his cell. For a moment, he remains alone. Then he breaks his magic staff and casts it away. Then he goes into the cell.

High up in the air, Ariel sings:

> Where the bee sucks, there suck I,
> In a cowslip's bell I lie;
> There I couch when owls do cry.
> On the bat's back I do fly
> After summer merrily.
> Merrily, merrily shall I live now,
> Under the blossom that hangs on the bough.

The curtain falls on the vessel that carries the king and his company back to Naples, and Prospero back to his dukedom, leaving Caliban to seek grace on the island.